The Psychosis Response Guide

Carina A. Iati, PsyD, is a licensed clinical psychologist in Boston, Massachusetts, where she provides psychological services to adolescents and young adults experiencing psychotic disorders in the Prevention and Recovery in Early Psychosis (PREP) Program at Massachusetts Mental Health Center. Dr. Iati provides individual, group, family, and multi-family therapy to assist young adults and their families in recovering from psychotic illnesses. She is an instructor in psychology in the Department of Psychiatry at Harvard Medical School and supervises psychology graduate students completing training in early psychosis treatment. Dr. Iati's research interests include early markers of schizophrenia spectrum disorders and personality assessment using the Minnesota Multiphasic Personality Inventory-2 (MMPI-2) and she has published several articles on these topics. She also teaches undergraduate courses in introductory psychology and abnormal psychology at Bunker Hill Community College, where she hopes to inspire the next generation of psychologists.

Rachel N. Waford, PhD, is a licensed clinical psychologist in Atlanta, Georgia. She is currently a supervising psychologist in the Department of Psychiatry at Emory University and a research assistant professor in Emory University's Rollins School of Public Health. Dr. Waford also has a part-time private practice specializing in individual and family treatment for severe mental illness, with an emphasis on early intervention for adolescents and young adults with psychosis. She is also involved with a number of community organizations in the Atlanta area to promote early intervention and recovery. A proponent of recovery in all forms, at all stages of the illness, Dr. Waford assists patients and families toward this goal.

The Psychosis Response Guide

How to Help Young People in Psychiatric Crises

Carina A. Iati, PsyD

Rachel N. Waford, PhD

SPRINGER PUBLISHING COMPANY

NEW YORK

Springer Publishing Company, LLC
11 West 42nd Street
New York, NY 10036
www.springerpub.com

Acquisitions Editor: Nancy S. Hale
Composition: Newgen KnowledgeWorks

ISBN: 978-0-8261-2437-1
e-book ISBN: 978-0-8261-2438-8

15 16 17 18 19 / 5 4 3 2 1

The author and the publisher of this Work have made every effort to use sources believed to be reliable to provide information that is accurate and compatible with the standards generally accepted at the time of publication. The author and publisher shall not be liable for any special, consequential, or exemplary damages resulting, in whole or in part, from the readers' use of, or reliance on, the information contained in this book. The publisher has no responsibility for the persistence or accuracy of URLs for external or third-party Internet websites referred to in this publication and does not guarantee that any content on such websites is, or will remain, accurate or appropriate.

Library of Congress Cataloging-in-Publication Data
Names: Iati, Carina A., author. | Waford, Rachel N., author.
Title: The psychosis response guide : how to help young people in psychiatric crises / Carina A. Iati, Rachel N. Waford.
Description: New York, NY: Springer Publishing Company, LLC, [2016] |
    Includes bibliographical references and index.
Identifiers: LCCN 2015037356 | ISBN 9780826124371 | ISBN 9780826124388 (e-book)
Subjects: | MESH: Adolescent. | Psychotic Disorders—therapy. |
    Schizophrenia—therapy. | Young Adult. | Crisis Intervention.
Classification: LCC RJ503 | NLM WS 463 | DDC 616.8900835—dc23
LC record available at http://lccn.loc.gov/2015037356

Printed in the United States of America by Gasch Printing.

This book is dedicated to all of the incredible young people we have had the pleasure to know and serve. It is inspired by the stories of recovery you embody. We hope that you will be proud of what we have created from the things you have taught us.

Contents

Foreword

This excellent book, *The Psychosis Response Guide: How to Help Young People in Psychiatric Crises*, fills an unmet need in the field of mental health treatment. There is now overwhelming evidence that the early detection and treatment of psychotic disorders are critical for optimizing prognosis. Yet, to date, there have been relatively few reference sources to assist professionals, friends, and families in navigating the road to diagnosis and early intervention. Moreover, among the books that are available, none is devoted to offering guidance primarily to those who are not in the field of mental health, yet are in a position to assist youth who are experiencing an initial episode of psychosis. There is no doubt that it is uniquely challenging to be confronted with the task of supporting and encouraging patients who are experiencing psychotic symptoms for the first time in their lives.

In this volume, Drs. Carina A. Iati and Rachel N. Waford offer expert and compassionate advice on recognizing the first signs of psychosis, as well as the strategies that professionals and friends and families can use to enhance the patient's entry into the treatment system. They offer solutions to the problems that are likely to emerge at each of the critical stages: engagement, intervention, and follow-up. The authors provide a thorough road map that addresses the characteristic features of these stages and the unique challenges that patients are likely to encounter in the journey to treatment and recovery. The authors' knowledge of our current scientific understanding of psychotic disorders, coupled with their clinical experience and sensitivity, makes this an extremely useful resource.

As the authors clearly document, there are unfortunate but significant differences between psychiatric and other medical disorders with respect to how their detection and treatment are conceptualized. Although there have been major advances in public education about mental health, social stigma and bias against those with psychiatric disorders remain. In fact, stigma is often the first barrier that individuals confront when they experience the onset of an initial psychotic episode. Seeking help and participating in treatment are still viewed by some as an admission of weakness or failure. Moving beyond this hurdle is necessary before the patient can fully engage in the diagnostic and treatment processes. Furthermore, the human nervous system is vastly more complex than any other organ system. As a result, our knowledge of both normal and dysfunctional brain processes is limited; to date, no specific brain region or mechanism has been linked with any specific psychiatric diagnosis. This can be daunting for patients who are seeking answers about etiology and treatments. And, of course, it makes the task of intervening to assist the individual in seeking treatment even more complex.

Nonetheless, as Drs. Iati and Waford describe, researchers have made progress and there are now effective treatments for virtually all psychiatric illnesses, including psychoses. In fact, the breadth of contemporary validated treatments for psychosis is impressive, and these span from psychotherapeutic, psychoeducational, and rehabilitative treatments to psychopharmacological regimens that can be tailored to address the patient's specific combination of symptoms.

There is no doubt that this book will be extremely helpful for those who work in fields such as education, law enforcement, and counseling, where there is an increased likelihood of encountering youth who are experiencing their first psychotic episode. The authors offer guidance that will be invaluable for professionals, authority figures, friends, and loved ones who are often struggling to engage in an honest conversation with a potential patient, while maintaining the integrity of their long-term relationship with the individual. Such conversations are never easy, and they can be even more difficult with a distressed young adult.

Having worked in the field of clinical research for more than 30 years, I have encountered numerous individuals who were confronted with the need to intervene on behalf of youth with emerging psychotic symptoms. This book is written by authors who are well aware that there is no single formula for such interventions, in that each situation presents unique conundrums. But there are viable strategies for optimizing the likelihood of a positive outcome, and Drs. Iati and Waford present compelling and informative examples of such encounters and excellent advice on how to navigate them. This book represents one more step in the direction of enhancing access to care for youth in need of mental health services. I expect that it will change many lives.

Elaine F. Walker, PhD
Samuel Candler Dobbs Professor of Psychology and Neuroscience
Emory University
Atlanta, Georgia

Preface

We are both excited to share this text and to assist in promoting recovery in young people with psychosis. We were drawn to individuals living with psychosis early in our training, and particularly affected by the opportunity to witness recovery in young people with psychosis. We valued getting to know them, being a part of their successes, and helping them build a foundation for recovery. We bonded over discussions of the unique appeal of this kind of work, as well as commiseration about the challenges and shortcomings of the way the mental health system presently serves teens and young adults with psychosis. Neither of us will hesitate to climb atop our soapbox and share idealistic notions of what we would like to see improve and how we could serve our clients better if only early intervention was a more broadly emphasized concept, if only young people were able to find services more quickly, if only more people had the tools to help.

Picking up on our enthusiasm and drive to better serve this community of patients, we decided to write this book together. We have been so fortunate to benefit from the wisdom of others; it was a challenge to believe we might have some of our own. This skepticism gave way to yet another idealistic conversation, where we found that, indeed, we do have something to share.

This book is drawn from the needs that we have observed, and our belief that all individuals experiencing psychosis deserve the opportunity for recovery. By offering you these tools, we believe it will allow such opportunities to occur more often. We believe that mental health care is not solely the concern of individuals with mental health conditions and providers who work within the mental health care system. Mental health should be a concern for every person who has other people in his or her life, in the same way that physical health is a priority. We do not hesitate to offer a Band-Aid to a friend who has a cut, to direct a feverish student to the nurse's office, or to sign the cast of a colleague with a broken arm.

Our aim is to offer you the tools to respond to a young adult with psychosis in the same way.

The majority of mental health texts are written keeping providers and patients in mind. *The Psychosis Response Guide: How to Help Young People in Psychiatric Crises* differs in that we envision a broader community, one that includes anyone who may be in the position to observe early signs of psychiatric crisis and initiate the first step toward treatment and future recovery. Thus, we hope that parents, teachers, friends, law enforcement officers, nurses, and school personnel will find this text relevant and useful. We firmly believe that *you* have the unique opportunity to initiate and impact steps toward recovery, hope, and a fulfilling life experience for a young adult in crisis. As clinicians and fellow community members, we would like to thank you in advance for considering and implementing the information we have included in this guide. We encourage you to share with friends and family the notion of recovery, changing the reputation of illnesses such as psychosis, and reducing the stigma of chronic mental illness.

Acknowledgments

This book was written with the help, support, and inspiration of many people. First and foremost, we want to thank our families and our friends for their encouragement while we took on this ambitious project. Their love and support make possible all of the work that we do, and this is no exception. We would like to thank our mentors, Dr. Rich Lewine and Dr. Kevin Bolinskey, who set us on the course toward doing this valuable work. We thank them for helping us build the foundation for this book, and for their continued encouragement as we take on increasing challenges. We would also like to thank Dr. Elaine F. Walker for her support of and participation in this project.

This book would not have been possible without Dr. Steve Walfish, who encouraged us to collaborate on this project and helped us find our voice to share the things that are most important to us. We cannot thank him enough for all of his support, both practical and personal.

Introduction: Mission and Purpose of This Book

The period from adolescence to young adulthood is characterized by abundant change and identity development. Unfortunately, it also marks the typical age of onset for many mental health concerns, including psychotic disorders. In recent years, we have begun to understand the importance of intervening early in mental illness in order to avoid a chronic and potentially disabling course. Imagine that you have broken your arm. How will it heal if you have it treated and casted immediately? What will happen if you wait 2 weeks to see if it will heal on its own? It will likely cause more pain and impairment in your daily life than if it were casted. What if you wait 4 years and it heals incorrectly? There may be irreversible damage that could have been avoided if the problem had been treated appropriately initially. Unfortunately, the mental health system has been treating psychiatric conditions in this way for some time, waiting until significant damage to a person's life or functioning has occurred before treatment is provided. Thankfully, this is beginning to change.

In recent years, there has been significant media attention paid to early detection of and intervention in psychotic illnesses. A number of tragic incidents have occurred in which the early stages of psychotic illness were implicated as a contributing factor. In some cases, it was reported that those in contact with the individual prior to the event had expressed concerns about the mental health condition of the offenders and suggested that they may have been experiencing a psychotic episode. These incidents are extreme circumstances, and are not representative of the behaviors of individuals with early psychosis, or psychosis in general. However, other tragedies occur on a less newsworthy scale every day as the symptoms of psychosis damage the academic and vocational careers, family relationships, social lives, and functional abilities of those who struggle with them. This book is intended to provide guidance to those who might notice changes in an individual and be unsure of how to respond.

Most often, the first people to notice symptoms of psychosis in a young adult are not mental health professionals who specialize in the treatment of psychosis. Rather, it is often the important people in the young person's life who take notice of the changing behavior, such as a teacher, guidance counselor, nurse, friend, parent, social worker, or primary care doctor. Alternatively, it may be someone who observes a concerning behavior but has no prior relationship with the individual, such as a police officer, a residence life counselor, or a concerned passerby. By taking notice of such behaviors all of these individuals have an opportunity to assist the young person and ideally help him or her to receive treatment.

We hope that this text is useful to a variety of audiences, although we acknowledge that each audience may have different strengths, limitations, and abilities to influence a young adult. For example, the experience of a friend offering advice and support is likely to be quite different from that of a campus police officer, and the way that a parent may notice changes in a young person's behavior is likely to be very different from changes that a professor may note. We hope that you will take the information provided in this book and view it through the lens of *your* relationship to the young adult you are trying to assist in order to be most effective in offering support and assistance.

These interactions are not easy; rather, they can be quite challenging and intimidating. We hope to provide a guide to demonstrate *how* to respond to these concerns in an effective manner. We hope to provide you with information and skills that will allow you to confidently and effectively interact with an individual experiencing psychosis, and to support him or her in accessing treatment. Through this text you will:

- Learn information about psychosis and related illnesses
- Develop an understanding of the benefits of early intervention in psychosis
- Develop skills for a successful interaction with a person with psychosis
- Learn strategies to support a young adult with psychosis in accessing treatment

The majority of this book focuses on fundamental knowledge, considerations, and examples to prepare you to intervene, all with the goal of the most effective interaction possible. If a troubled individual is brought to your attention, then we encourage you to follow the steps we have laid out for you to assist the person in connecting and engaging with treatment. We understand that from that initial determination that someone may need help, the path is largely unknown. There are many paths, in fact, and many predictable and unpredictable challenges and barriers along the way. Although we always hope for the best-case scenario, it is important to acknowledge that this may not always be possible. In some cases, we may intervene simply with the hope of reducing the likelihood of harm to the young person or others. Our goal is to arm you with tools to maneuver around challenges and barriers in the best possible way to facilitate engagement with care. This may not always be the outcome, but that is the goal.

The techniques and strategies outlined in this book will be conveyed through the lens of a "better safe than sorry" approach. We discuss safety (potential harm to self or others) at many different points in this text, and reiterate the need to take a conservative approach to responding to safety concerns. Although this may seem heavy-handed at times, safety is the foremost concern in such situations and we believe that it is better to respond too conservatively than to withhold a response when it is needed. Thus, regarding safety concerns, when in doubt call 911. The "better safe than sorry" approach also generally encourages an attempt at engagement and initiating a conversation about some form of help if any concerns about psychiatric symptoms arise. Returning to our broken arm analogy, if you thought your arm was broken wouldn't you go get it checked out either way, just to be sure?

Your intervention and support could make a world of difference in the life of a young person with a psychotic illness. Such illnesses were once considered hopelessly chronic, with little confidence in treatment or improvement beyond medication. However, now we know that recovery is possible, particularly with early intervention strategies. Your supportive actions may very well change the course of an individual's life for the better. You are reading this text because you might be in a position to assist a young adult experiencing psychosis. This is both an empowering and intimidating place to be. By using this text we hope that you will be able to enter such an interaction with confidence and appropriate caution, having the tools and the knowledge to provide assistance.

We are inspired to write this text by the experiences we have had working with young adults with psychotic illnesses. As licensed psychologists with training in early psychosis, we have had the opportunity to work with many amazing young people and their families and have learned a tremendous amount from them. We have seen recovery in its many forms. We have seen young people return to school and work, develop meaningful relationships, rebuild their confidence, achieve their goals, and become mental health advocates themselves. We have seen people work very hard to feel better than they did yesterday, to manage their own medications successfully, to stay out of the hospital, or to reduce conflict with their family. Recovery is an individual journey, and each step toward a better life is valuable. We have also seen the difficulty that our young people face in accessing treatment for psychosis. Many individuals experience months or even years of psychotic illness before coming to the attention of a specialized mental health care provider and receiving appropriate treatment. We hope to bring these experiences to this text in a way that will both inform and inspire you to become a vehicle for change in a young person's life. We invite you to join our efforts to create more stories of recovery and success, and continue to demonstrate that early intervention can change lives.

CHAPTER **ONE**

What Do We Know About Schizophrenia Spectrum Disorders and Treatment Options?

As we have discussed, the first people to notice changes in a young adult's behavior that might be indicative of psychosis are often not specialists on the subject. Instead, they are well-meaning people in the young person's life who care about his or her well-being. Although it is not necessary to be knowledgeable or trained in mental health in order to assist, we believe that some foundational information can be very helpful in identifying a time, place, and effective method of intervention. This chapter broadly describes psychotic illness, theories and models of illness development, and prevalence rates. Treatments for psychotic disorders are also discussed, followed by substantial and robust evidence for early intervention and support from policy initiatives. The material is intended to be informational rather than a prerequisite to providing assistance to someone in need. Due to the nature of the content, this chapter contains much more "jargon" than other chapters. Please do not be intimidated. The goal is not to be able to "diagnose" someone or to develop a complete understanding of the academic literature on psychosis, but rather to develop a basic understanding of psychotic illnesses as a foundation, and gain a better understanding of the experiences of individuals you may have the opportunity to assist.

DIAGNOSING MENTAL ILLNESS

Psychotic disorders are a category of illnesses classified as mental illness. In general, a mental illness is a medical condition that disrupts a person's thinking, feeling, mood, ability to relate to others, and daily functioning (National Alliance on Mental Illness, 2015). Mental illnesses can affect anyone regardless of age, race, ethnicity, gender, socioeconomic status, education level, religion, or sexual orientation. Although these illnesses can significantly impact lives in a variety of challenging ways, many individuals can, and do, recover. Like any medical condition, mental illnesses are diagnosed using a preidentified group of symptoms, or *criteria*, that have shown to be disproportionately common in a certain experience. For instance, feelings of hopelessness, difficulty sleeping, and thoughts of suicide are more common in individuals experiencing depression than those who are not. Thus, these are part of the criteria for diagnosing depression. Many of the most common and most severe mental illnesses have been identified for centuries, and there is considerable evidence regarding what symptoms, when occurring together, are indicative of a particular type of problem.

Just as there are categories of other physical illnesses that encompass specific diagnoses (e.g., infectious diseases, pulmonary problems, endocrine problems), there are categories of psychiatric illnesses (e.g., psychotic disorders, anxiety disorders, eating disorders). Psychiatric illnesses are identified by licensed mental health providers who are trained in diagnosis, assessment, and intervention. These professionals include psychologists, psychiatrists, social workers, and mental health or professional counselors. Some individuals experiencing psychosis for the first time may be initially identified by their general practitioner or primary care provider, but should also be formally diagnosed and treated by a mental health professional. Licensed mental health treatment providers can be found in a variety of settings: hospitals, community mental health centers, college counseling centers, and primary care offices, to name a few.

WHAT ARE PSYCHOTIC DISORDERS?

The term *psychotic disorder* refers to a continuum of illness that encompasses a variety of different symptoms. "Continuum" in this context refers to the significant variation that exists from "normal" experience to "abnormal" experience. In fact, most, if not all, psychiatric illnesses exist on a continuum. This means that most people at one time or another, and under certain conditions, can experience a number of psychiatric symptoms. What differentiate a diagnosable illness from the normal variation of human experience are the severity, duration, and prolonged impact of the symptom(s) on the individual (Figure 1.1).

Mental illness, just like other medical illnesses, includes symptoms that are deviations from what *most* healthy people experience, *most* of the time. Importantly, this does not include experiences or behaviors that are innate to a particular culture and thus have meaning for one cultural group but not another. Cultural-bound experiences and behaviors are not considered symptoms of mental illness even if *most* people do not experience or understand them. Outside of that caveat, we all have strange or aberrant experiences every now and then; for example, we hear our phone ringing when it has not or believe we see an object out of the corner of our eye when nothing is there. However, certain recurring, persistent patterns or clusters of symptoms that cause problems in daily life typically indicate a particular condition or disorder. Psychotic disorders are identified by a number of characteristic symptoms: positive symptoms (e.g., hallucinations and delusions); negative symptoms (e.g., low motivation and limited emotional expression); disorganized speech/thought (e.g., thought disorder); disorganized behavior (e.g., inappropriate laughter); cognitive impairments; and affective symptoms. "Positive" and "negative" in this context do not refer to "good" or "bad" experiences. Instead, they reflect the added *presence* and notable *absence* of experiences, respectively. These symptoms are covered at length in Chapter 2.

Significant variation, known as *heterogeneity*, exists within and across psychotic disorders; a multitude of symptom combinations are possible that can still meet criteria for one of the disorders. This means that two people with schizophrenia, for example, can have two very different combinations and/or presentations of symptoms but still meet the criteria for having the same diagnosis. Essentially, not all people with schizophrenia

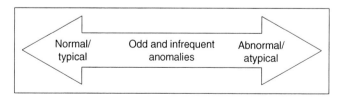

Normal/
typical

Odd and infrequent
anomalies

Abnormal/
atypical

FIGURE 1.1
Continuum arrow.

are alike. The *Diagnostic and Statistical Manual of Mental Disorders*, fifth edition (*DSM-5*; American Psychiatric Association [APA], 2013) classifies all psychotic disorders under the umbrella of *schizophrenia spectrum disorders* to account for the differences that occur within and between psychotic disorders. In addition to significant symptom differences under the umbrella of psychotic disorders, there are also differences in the prevalence rates of the different psychotic disorders. Prevalence rates indicate how frequently the illness occurs or, said another way, the proportion of individuals diagnosed with the illness at a given time. Table 1.1 displays names and prevalence rates of the various psychotic disorders as well as a summary of symptoms. Please note that the symptoms in Table 1.1 are not a complete list of criteria, but rather are a simplified guide to the most notable features of each illness. A more complete description of the various symptoms is presented in Chapter 2. Of the different diagnoses, schizophrenia is found in approximately 1% of the population in the United States (National Institute of Mental Health [NIMH], 2009). Said a different way, it is estimated that one person in every 100 people will be diagnosed with schizophrenia.

Before moving forward let us pause for a moment. An important distinction exists between a psychotic *episode* and a psychotic *disorder*. As the name suggests, a psychotic *episode* is an acute experience of psychotic symptoms with a somewhat distinct "beginning" or exacerbation period, and an "end" or remission period. Episodes can occur only once, or multiple times. Often, individuals who experience multiple psychotic episodes will have periods between episodes in which they experience few or no symptoms. Psychotic *disorders* develop when there is a recurrence of symptoms. That is, the individual has experienced several episodes and these experiences cause distress in a number of important areas of his or her life, namely occupational (e.g., work or school); social (e.g., friends, family, coworkers, and social situations in general); and/or adaptive functioning (e.g., taking care of oneself and personal hygiene). In addition, the identification of a disorder requires meeting criteria for a specified duration (how long the symptoms have persisted), number of symptoms present, combination of symptoms present, and severity of impact on functioning. It is largely differences across these four domains that distinguish psychotic disorders, and discern psychotic disorders as a whole from other illnesses with similar symptoms.

Individuals who have been diagnosed with a psychotic disorder often have episodes where shifts occur from a period of decreased symptoms (e.g., remission and stability) to a period of increased symptoms (e.g., relapse, exacerbation, and decompensation) in response to some trigger or life stressor. Examples of common triggers or life stressors include relationship problems, academic hardships, or change in environment.

TABLE 1.1

Symptom Profiles and Prevalence Rates for Psychotic Disorders

Disorders	Prevalence Information[a]	Summary of Symptoms
Schizophrenia	~1% of the general population	• Positive symptoms • Negative symptoms • Disorganization often present • Duration of symptoms *more* than 6 months
Schizophreniform disorder	Incidence appears low, but may be as common as schizophrenia	• Positive symptoms • Negative symptoms • Disorganization often present • Duration of symptoms *less* than 6 months
Bipolar disorder with psychotic features	0.6% of the general population for bipolar disorder in general. Addition of psychotic features is even less common	• At least one episode of mania • Episodes of depressed mood • Positive symptoms of psychosis only when mania or depressive mood symptoms are present • Negative symptoms may or may not be present
Schizoaffective disorder	Estimated 0.3% of the general population	• Positive symptoms • Negative symptoms • Positive and negative symptoms are present even when not experiencing a manic or depressive episode
Depression with psychotic features	7% of the general population for depression in general. Less common with psychotic features	• Episodes of depression • Symptoms of psychosis only when depressed mood symptoms are present • Negative symptoms may or may not be present

[a]Prevalence information describes data in the United States and is provided by the *Diagnostic and Statistical Manual of Mental Disorders,* fifth edition (APA, 2013).

Often, recurrences of symptoms are related to environmental stressors. For instance, starting a new job, moving, or the end of a relationship are environmental stressors that could lead symptoms to reemerge, exacerbate current symptoms that had been manageable, and increase the likelihood of an episode. In other cases, an episode may be triggered by some biological change that takes place: for example, the introduction of a substance, such as marijuana, cocaine, alcohol, or some commonly prescribed medication, to the individual's system. Or, if an individual discontinues prescribed medication that was biologically treating symptoms, symptoms may emerge. These changes alter the way a person's brain chemistry works, and for individuals who experience psychosis these changes may increase vulnerability to a recurrence of symptoms. Although these examples describe events that are often related to psychotic episodes, it is possible for an episode to occur without any discernible cause. For instance, symptoms may slowly and subtly emerge over time without being an identifiable trigger or change.

It is also important to note that there are many other illnesses that include the same or similar symptoms. However, the origin or cause of the specific symptoms is of critical importance for diagnosis and subsequent treatment; the origin of the psychotic symptom will determine the best and most appropriate course of action for a mental health or medical

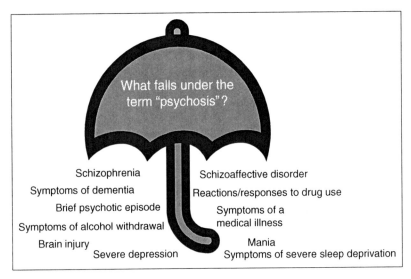

FIGURE 1.2
Variety of illnesses with psychosis.

provider. Identifying the many possible origins of psychotic symptoms is beyond the scope of this book as that is not the responsibility of the "first responder." However, it may be helpful for general consideration and knowledge. Figure 1.2 displays the variety of medical and psychiatric illnesses that include psychotic symptoms, and examples of these illnesses and "differential diagnoses" are discussed in Chapter 2.

CAUSES AND PRECIPITANTS OF PSYCHOTIC ILLNESS

Although it is not necessary to understand why someone is displaying psychotic symptoms in order to intervene, the information can be helpful when coordinating a referral plan. Moreover, understanding the etiology of these disorders can also provide a context for the specific episode and increase empathy on the part of those who may be in a position to help.

There are two important factors that contribute to the development of a psychotic disorder: genetics/heredity, and stress or trauma. The genetic and biological underpinnings of the various psychotic disorders may vary, and an in-depth discussion of each illness is beyond the scope of this text. However, in order to illustrate the role of heredity, let us consider schizophrenia spectrum disorders as an exemplar. Schizophrenia spectrum disorders are highly heritable. This means that if one immediate relative (e.g., mother or father) is living with a schizophrenia spectrum disorder, then it is *more likely* that a child of that person will develop a psychotic illness. The child may also be more vulnerable to developing another illness shown to be highly associated with psychotic illness. The heritability level decreases as you move away from first-degree relatives and into extended family members (aunt, uncle, grandparent, and so on). For example, it is *less* likely that you will develop schizophrenia if your aunt was diagnosed with schizophrenia than if your mother was diagnosed with schizophrenia, and *more* likely than if your third cousin has been diagnosed with schizophrenia. The heritability of schizophrenia spectrum disorders is also known as a "genetic vulnerability" for the illness.

Although the genetics of schizophrenia spectrum and associated disorders is beyond the scope of this book, there is evidence that schizophrenia may be genetically linked to or associated with other disorders such as schizotypal personality disorder, autism-spectrum disorders, bipolar and depressive disorders, and attention deficit hyperactivity disorder (ADHD; Cardno & Owen, 2014; Craddock, O'Donovan, & Owe, 2009; Cross-Disorder Group of the Psychiatric

Genomics Consortium, 2013). Because of the strong genetic link to other disorders, these associated disorders are also more prevalent in the first-degree relatives of individuals diagnosed with schizophrenia. For example, the child of an individual diagnosed with schizophrenia is more likely to develop a bipolar disorder or ADHD than someone else who does not have a family member with schizophrenia. The study of the genetics of schizophrenia is a very "hot topic" right now, with significant scientific research funds dedicated to identifying a gene(s) that may cause or increase the likelihood of schizophrenia spectrum disorders. However, to date, there is no "schizophrenia gene." Rather, schizophrenia is considered to be a polygenic disorder, meaning that several genes are proposed to interact to increase vulnerability (Tsuang, Stone, Tarbox, & Faraone, 2002).

Experiencing stress or trauma also increases the likelihood that someone may develop a schizophrenia spectrum disorder. "Trauma" can refer to occurrences of abuse in childhood (experienced or witnessed), extreme violence, significant loss, or other serious threats of harm or safety. Whether increased number of traumas alone significantly increases risk has yet to be determined. However, evidence exists that individuals exposed to traumatic experiences appear to be at greater risk for developing a psychotic illness (Addington et al., 2013; Bechdolf et al., 2010; Thompson et al., 2014). Additionally, it is more likely that someone who experienced a trauma in childhood may have future difficulty coping with anxiety, stressors, or other problematic events if proper treatment and support are not provided (Van Winkel et al., 2013).

In addition to trauma, experiencing stress is also significantly related to developing a psychotic illness. As we all know, stress comes in many forms and in varying levels of severity. Minor stressors include circumstances such as sitting in traffic, meeting deadlines, and relationship conflict. Major stressors include loss, hormonal changes, significant medical illnesses, moving/relocation, and other life changes (anticipated and unanticipated). Positive stress can also occur and be equally overwhelming. Getting a new job, inheriting a large sum of money, having a child, and starting college are all examples of exciting life experiences that can be difficult and stressful. Although this is explored in more detail later in the text, this review of stressors highlights the importance of early intervention in adolescence through young adulthood as there are a myriad of changes and stressors (positive and negative) occurring during this period, thus creating one of the most vulnerable periods for developing any psychiatric illness. Notably, the most severe and persistent mental illnesses are characterized by their onset during this period (e.g., schizophrenia spectrum illnesses, bipolar illnesses, and borderline personality disorder; Mantt et al., 2013; Sturman & Moghaddam, 2011). Now, let us be careful here. Experiencing a significant trauma or traumas does not mean that someone will then become psychotic. Nor is it meant to imply that those who experience a lot of stress are more likely to develop a psychotic disorder. It is *typically* a combination of factors that contribute to increased vulnerability, and ultimately development of a psychotic disorder. The most well-known model of the development of schizophrenia spectrum disorders is the diathesis-stress model (Falconer, 1965; Fowles, 1992; Gottesman & Shields, 1967). The diathesis-stress model, or stress-vulnerability model as it is otherwise known, suggests that a combination of genetic vulnerability and stress creates the most significant risk for developing a psychotic illness. Individuals with a first-degree relative diagnosed with a schizophrenia spectrum illness and thus a higher genetic vulnerability for developing the illness themselves have a lower threshold for stress or trauma that can promote development of the illness. An illustration of this fact based on the model is given as follows (Brabban & Turkington, 2002). See Figure 1.3 for a pictorial version.

> Imagine that we are all born with a bucket. Imagine that individuals with no family history of schizophrenia spectrum illness have a gallon bucket and can hold or "withstand" a gallon's worth of water/volume/stress. On the other hand, imagine that individuals who do have a genetic risk for developing a schizophrenia spectrum illness or psychotic disorder have a half-gallon bucket. Now, imagine that all of the stressors that we can experience in a given day or time period (e.g., traffic, financial problems, more demanding work or school load, family arguments, graduating from high school, losing a job) are represented by drops of water. An individual's personal bucket determines what they can hold. From the start, individuals with a half-gallon bucket are at a disadvantage as their buckets hold less than those without a genetic vulnerability. The bucket gets filled faster, and is more likely to overflow. For those at risk for developing a psychotic illness (i.e., genetic vulnerability), the "overflow" can signify a first psychotic episode, and is a consistent pattern for future episodes.

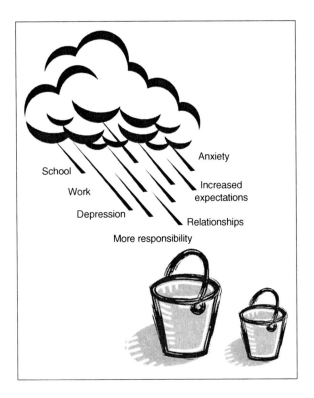

FIGURE 1.3
Stress-vulnerability model.

Thankfully, there are "sponges," otherwise known as treatments, supports, and other factors that "soak up" some of the stress to reduce overflow and keep everything at a manageable level.

TREATMENTS FOR PSYCHOTIC ILLNESS

Medication

There are several interventions that have been shown to be effective for treating and promoting recovery in schizophrenia. Depending on the individual, varying combinations of the empirically supported interventions may be effective in treating the illness. The first-line treatment is often medication. Antipsychotic medications are designed to correct chemical imbalances in the brain that contribute to psychotic symptoms. These medications largely treat the positive symptoms (e.g., hallucinations and delusions that may be present) of psychosis and were first developed in the 1950s, with the first efficacious treatment found for Thorazine in 1952 (Carpenter & Davis, 2012). Although the first antipsychotic medications known as "typicals" (e.g., Haldol and Thorazine) had a significant impact on symptom reduction, they had acute side effects for some individuals such as tremors and involuntary movements, extreme restlessness, and spasms in different areas of the body (Carpenter & Davis, 2012). These side effects can also persist long term. To combat side effects and associated medication nonadherence, a new wave of antipsychotics were developed called "atypicals." These medications (e.g., Seroquel, Risperdal, Clozaril, and Zyprexa) have fewer side effects and have the ability to impact a wider range of symptoms such as mood symptoms. Both types of antipsychotic medications are used today in combination with other medications (e.g., antidepressants, mood stabilizers, antianxiety medications) to reduce side effects. Similar to other pharmacological treatments, finding the right medication "match" is an individualized and, at times, laborious process. However, the benefits of a century of research have led to medications that significantly reduce symptoms and considerably improve quality of life for individuals with psychotic disorders.

Other medications such as antidepressants, mood stabilizers, and anxiolytics (antianxiety) medications are often used to decrease significant mood symptoms that often accompany the illness. Mood symptoms may be the result of (a) the symptoms of schizophrenia, (b) stressors directly and indirectly related to having a mental illness, or (c) an additional mental illness that exacerbates and is exacerbated by schizophrenia. No matter the cause of the mood symptom, medications designed to regulate or stabilize mood are complementary to antipsychotic medications (McRenolds, Mehta, & Nasrallah, 2013).

Psychotherapy

Psychotherapy is the second most recommended treatment for psychotic disorders and is often recommended as adjunctive treatment for all individuals with these diagnoses (McRenolds et al., 2013). Psychotherapy comes in three major modalities: individual therapy, group therapy, and family therapy. These three modalities are often used in conjunction with one another to address multiple domains affected by psychosis. There are a myriad of empirically supported therapies that are available, although some have more support for schizophrenia than others. Table 1.2 presents

TABLE 1.2

Psychosocial Treatments for Schizophrenia

Treatment	Approach	Symptom Focus	Reference
Cognitive behavioral therapy for psychosis	Individual or group therapy focused on modifying and restructuring cognitions and emotional responses	• Positive symptoms • Negative symptoms • Associated psychosocial challenges	Rathod, Kingdon, Weiden, & Turkington (2008)

Cognitive remediation/ cognitive enhancement therapy	Paper-and-pencil tests and/or computerized exercises targeting specific cognitive domains	• Cognitive deficits
		  – Memory
		  – Attention
		  – Motor speed
		• Cognitive enhancement therapy also addresses social cognition deficits
			Cella, Huddy, Reeder, & Wykes (2012); Hogarty & Flesher (1999)

Family therapies	Individual, group, and/or support group therapy formats	• Psychoeducation • Crisis intervention • Effective support • Family coping	Lehman et al. (2004); Pilling et al. (2002)
Psychodynamic psychotherapy	Individual therapy	Unconscious emotions and motivations that may be related to symptom presentation	Leichsenring & Leibing (2007)

Psychosocial rehabilitation	Individual and group-based interventions are integrated in a comprehensive treatment model	Addresses recovery in multiple domains: • Social skills • Supported employment • Environmental support • Family intervention	Kopelowicz, Liberman, & Wallace (2003)
Social skills training	Individual and group therapy approaches incorporating modeling, role-playing, corrective feedback, and community-based activities	Deficits in: • Social perception • Social awareness • Social expression	Kurtz & Mueser (2008)

the most common treatments for schizophrenia, their approach, the targeted symptom(s), and references for more information. Across interventions, individual therapy has shown to be effective for increasing understanding of symptoms, teaching and strengthening methods of coping with symptoms and stressors, providing interpersonal connection and support, and stimulating motivation for treatment (Addington, Piskulic, & Marshall, 2010; Hamm, Hasson-Ohayon, Kukla, & Lysaker, 2013; Lockwood, Page, & Conroy-Hiller, 2004; Morrison, 2009). Individual psychotherapy also promotes insight into illness, a trait that has been asserted to be predictive of recovery and success (Amador & David, 2004).

Group therapy has shown to be highly effective in addressing symptoms and stressors associated with psychotic disorders. This approach decreases feelings of isolation and provides support from peers with a shared experience. A common symptom associated with psychosis is decreased social skills and limited social awareness. Training of social skills has shown to be effective in improving social deficits (Kurtz & Mueser, 2008) and group therapy provides a wonderful opportunity to practice and refine these skills, as well as an opportunity to watch others "model" more appropriate skills.

Family therapy is a third commonly used approach for psychotherapy for psychotic disorders. As you might expect, psychosis impacts more than just the individual; all personal and professional relationships are affected to some degree. For family members and caregivers, the impact is huge. Family members and caregivers experience significant confusion, guilt, isolation, fear, anger, and sadness. These experiences are associated with concern about their loved one, mourning over "lost potential" or what their loved one "could have been," and the burden of navigating the health care system and managing a very difficult illness. Not surprisingly, these thoughts and feelings can introduce a number of relationship challenges within the family. As discussed earlier, challenges or stressors often exacerbate symptoms of psychosis, promoting a very difficult and painful cycle. Thus, family therapy includes education for family members and caregivers, the teaching of methods of coping and self-care, developing strategies for improved communication, and support, among other elements characteristic of specific family therapy approaches. Family therapy can occur in an individual format (e.g., one family) or in a group setting where multiple families come together and work with a clinician facilitating a particular treatment. Many families decide to participate in both types of family therapy.

Rehabilitative Therapies

Psychotic disorders are debilitating in many different areas. In addition to the confusing and terrifying symptoms experienced by individuals living with the illness and the interpersonal problems that result from multiple challenges, individuals with psychosis also suffer from decreased functioning at school and work. In the early stages of the illness (adolescence through young adulthood), individuals may have to leave school, quit jobs, or miss out on critical opportunities for education and training that often occur during this developmental period. Moreover, these individuals may experience a loss of skills caused by cognitive impairment such as memory problems and poor concentration and focus, requiring a period of relearning or retraining. As an individual is moving toward recovery, missed educational and vocational opportunities can also be a stressful experience, which can exacerbate psychotic symptoms. Vocational and occupational training has been shown to be an extremely beneficial intervention for these individuals when added to other empirically supported treatments. Vocational and occupational treatments include job training programs, academic preparation programs, and focus on skills such as communication skills, organization, time management, and planning.

Treatment Settings

Treatment can occur in a variety of settings. Many individuals living with a psychotic disorder will experience treatment in multiple settings over the course of their illness. Inpatient treatment is reserved for episodes where individuals are at risk of harming themselves or others. Although each state differs with regard to its laws on involuntary hospitalization, people are typically admitted to a psychiatric unit (voluntarily or involuntarily) when there is concern that they may be at risk for harm and demonstrate decreased ability to regulate their impulses, and when there is concern about their ability to care for themselves (e.g., shelter, safety, eating). Hospital admissions vary from state to state and facility to facility. Longer admissions may be necessary for more severe episodes, managing and monitoring medication changes, and establishing safe treatment plans. Partial hospitalization programs are intensive treatment settings designed to ease the transition from an inpatient setting and 24-hour supervision to outpatient treatment. Although the programs may vary, a partial hospital program often includes an intensive treatment program during the entire day (e.g., combination of individual and group therapy) and returning at night to home or a supervised living facility.

Outpatient treatment occurs in a variety of settings including private practice offices, community clinics, and day treatment and psychosocial rehabilitation programs. Depending on the treatment plan and level of care necessary, outpatient care may occur weekly, biweekly, or daily such as a day treatment program. Day treatment programs and psychosocial rehabilitation programs include scheduled programming providing a combination of individual therapy, group therapy, and rehabilitation treatment. These programs also provide a built-in support system with peers and staff working together to promote and achieve recovery. Day treatment and psychosocial rehabilitation programs also typically have established relationships with other community-based programs and thus can provide many unique opportunities for teaching, learning, and networking. Overall, their mission is to help promote reintegration into the community.

SUPPORT FOR EARLY INTERVENTION

Research to Date

The support for early intervention for severe mental illness is long-standing and robust. Although many individuals with psychosis will continue to have residual symptoms over the course of their lifetimes, early intervention decreases the likelihood of a life with a chronic and debilitating illness, and contributes to improved quality of life and pursuit of life's many opportunities. The longer the duration of untreated illness, the more difficult the recovery process can be (Hongyun et al., 2014). Without early identification and early intervention, the process is lengthier and much more challenging. Meanwhile, during a period of untreated illness, individuals lose important functionalities, become disconnected from friends and loved ones, experience confusion and shame, experience significant psychosocial stress, and battle very debilitating symptoms. Individuals living with psychosis also have an increased risk of suicide. It has been estimated that approximately one third of individuals with schizophrenia will attempt suicide, and approximately 10% of individuals will take their life (Centers for Disease Control and Prevention, 2014; NIMH, 2009).

Luckily, seminal research has demonstrated that when treatment is introduced at the earliest signs of illness, most individuals with psychotic disorders are able to achieve a fulfilling and purposeful life. There is no identifiable cure for schizophrenia or psychosis at this time, meaning that most individuals will not be entirely free from symptoms even when stable. However, treatments focus on recovery rather than cure. *Recovery* entails symptom management, effective coping strategies, and pursuit of individual goals. Problems that are identified and treated early in the illness typically have better outcomes, as individuals (a) learn effective strategies for coping with current and future episodes; (b) understand and reduce "triggers" for relapse and decompensation; and (c) become contributing members of society (Mueser, Deavers, Penn, & Cassisi, 2013). Learning new, effective coping strategies provides options for managing psychotic symptoms and combating associated feelings such as depression, anxiety, and fear. Although antipsychotic medications can provide quick relief from some of the positive symptoms of psychosis, they often do not completely resolve. In this case, effective coping and insight into illness are particularly important in assisting an individual with managing residual symptoms. Moreover, other challenges may arise as individuals gain more understanding about having a lifelong illness. Although the mantra "knowledge is power" suggests that knowing more is better, it does not mean that knowing more is *easier*. In fact, greater insight into having a psychotic disorder can be very difficult. Frequently, individuals in the early stages of chronic illness experience depression, hopelessness, or loss of motivation related to their newly diagnosed condition. Thus, early intervention focused on coping skills introduces a number of strategies for managing troubling thoughts and feelings about an individual's circumstance. Common strategies include distraction techniques, identifying how and where to seek support from others, physical activities to reduce stress, maintaining healthy behaviors, and learning how to restructure negative thinking patterns.

In addition to learning how to cope with stress and challenging symptoms and circumstances, early interventions geared toward understanding triggers and warning signs for a psychotic episode have shown to be immensely helpful in introducing a greater feeling of control over an individual's experience. The manifestation of psychotic symptoms is unique in many ways. Certain situations or stimuli may trigger or increase the likelihood of a psychotic episode. Moreover, stressful situations, which may also be unique to the individual, can bring about symptoms of psychosis. Triggers can be even more specific and detailed. For example, an individual may not be easily bothered by an argument with a sister, but may be particularly sensitive to an argument with his or her mother. In another patient, it may be just the opposite. When individuals learn and understand situations and patterns that increase their personal vulnerability, they are better able to implement coping strategies and stave off a psychotic episode. The rationale is similar for understanding personal warning signs. It is common for individuals with psychotic disorders to have physical and psychological indicators of an episode. This can be manifested in many unique ways and may include an increase in a particular symptom (e.g., delusion or hallucination); decrease in an area of functioning (e.g., poor sleep or not completing schoolwork); or physical sensations (e.g., heart palpitations or muscle tension). The earlier someone is able to understand these individualized experiences, the more likely he or she is to be successful at managing the illness in the future.

Finally, identifying personal goals and rebuilding confidence are critical to achieving recovery. This can be achieved in a variety of ways and may look different from an individual's original "life plan" before the onset of illness. No matter the recovery plan, feeling successful is an important part of the recovery process. When individuals feel more in control of their thoughts, feelings, and behaviors, and feel confident in their ability to pursue and achieve goals, they are more likely to engage in society in a way that is beneficial for the individual and the community at large. This may include returning to school, getting a job, volunteering with a local organization, or developing a healthy and fulfilling hobby. When an individual feels more confident and in control, and is in pursuit of goals, he or she is less vulnerable to triggers for psychosis, and is more likely to participate in effective intervention.

Crunching the Numbers

Mental illness is a costly business. In 2003, the World Health Organization (WHO) estimated that schizophrenia was the second most costly illness, with more than $15,000 spent per patient each year in the United States (WHO, 2003; Figure 1.4). Although mental illness is a personal challenge, it is also a public health issue as benefits of early intervention have broad impact on taxpayer dollars. Research has shown that early intervention for psychosis is associated with better recovery trajectories as evidenced by return to school or work, significantly fewer future episodes and hospital admissions, and reduced caregiver burden (WHO, 2003). Not surprisingly, delayed intervention results in lengthier and more frequent hospital admissions, increased contact with the legal system, and increased vulnerability to other costly public health issues such as homelessness, substance abuse, and comorbid medical issues (Insel, 2008). Tax dollars pay for state psychiatric hospital care, mental health care in prisons, and many other social intervention programs that target these problems (e.g., homelessness). Chronic sufferers of psychosis are often unable to "pay in" to the system due to lost educational and economic opportunities, leaving the incurring of costs to caregivers and public programs paid for by federal, state, and local dollars. To be more precise, serious mental illness costs the United States $193.2 billion annually in lost earnings (Insel, 2008). The best chance for reducing the illness burden is early intervention at the first signs of possible symptoms or illness before functionalities are lost. There is significant empirical support for early intervention, with considerable benefits for the individual and for society at large. When left to progress and persist, mental illness, and specifically psychosis, leads to substantial burden and harm. Introducing intervention at the earliest signs of difficulty has positive, impactful results for everyone.

Dedicated Research Programs

Thankfully, there are clinical research endeavors dedicated to increasing early identification and intervention efforts. Two examples of funded clinical research studies in the United States are the North American Prodrome Longitudinal Study (NAPLS; Addington et al., 2012) and the Recovery After an Initial Schizophrenia Episode (RA1SE; NIMH, 2009) project. NAPLS aims to improve prediction rates (e.g., who is most likely to develop a psychotic illness) and identify factors that contribute to increased risk of developing a psychotic illness (e.g., biological and behavioral aberrations or changes). RA1SE seeks to promote change in the course of a developed psychotic illness through intensive and coordinated treatment in the early stages of the illness. In addition to these larger, multisite intervention studies, there is a myriad of smaller clinics across the United States dedicated to early identification and intervention. This approach also has international support with large, comprehensive treatment studies for early identification and prevention of psychotic illness in a number of countries including Australia (Early Psychosis Prevention and Intervention Centre [EPPIC]; McGorry, Edwards, Mihalopoulos, Harrigan, & Jackson, 1996) and Scandinavia (The European Prediction of Psychosis Study [EPOS]; Ruhrmann et al., 2010).

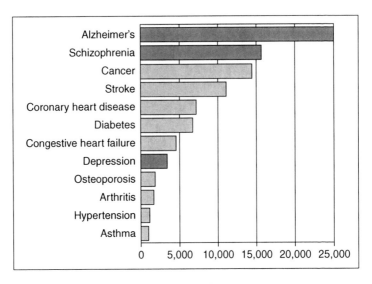

FIGURE 1.4
The yearly cost per patient for schizophrenia and other selected medical
conditions: United States U.S.$/patient/year.
Source: WHO, 2003.

A Policy Shift

On January 17, 2014, President Barack Obama signed into law the
Consolidated Appropriations Act of 2014. In response to an outcry
for greater emphasis on mental health treatment following a series of
violent tragedies at the hands of young people with a history of distress, the U.S. government declared that "Now Is the Time" and provided funds to the Substance Abuse and Mental Health Services
Administration (SAMHSA) to support development of programs
geared toward early identification and treatment for psychosis. In collaboration with the NIMH, evidence-based treatment models have been
implemented and examined in clinical care centers across the country.
Ninety-nine million dollars in grant funding was allocated for specialized training of mental health providers, developing of policies
to improve safety in schools, and increasing access to mental health
resources.

Why Are You So Vital to This Process?

We have learned that early intervention for psychosis is critical for achieving recovery and a fulfilling life. The period of development when psychosis often develops (adolescence through young adulthood) can be chaotic and confusing with lots of changes happening at once. Luckily, this stage includes participation in a number of environments where changes can be monitored over time. These include school, home with family, organized sports, and community programs. If you are reading this book, then you are likely a professional in one of these environments and have a unique opportunity to notice and monitor troubling changes displayed by an individual. All too often, someone does not reach a clinician's door until after an extended period of difficulty and decline, and at times after escalation of symptoms has led to hospitalization or arrest. In hindsight, we are often able to identify a number of characteristic issues that suggest that the problems began some time ago.

The next chapter distinguishes *typical* and *expected* changes from atypical and concerning changes that most often occur during adolescence and young adulthood. We are asking you to take note of statements, behaviors, and alterations that appear to be falling outside of the typical range and may be cause for alarm. We are not asking you to become mental health experts or are we suggesting that you become a responsible party in the future of someone's care. However, we are requesting your help by asking you to acknowledge your unique role and huge capacity to facilitate access to care. We hope there will be more "false alarms" than not, but we also know that not acting or intervening can have detrimental effects for someone who *is* at risk for developing a psychotic illness. Moving forward we will be encouraging a "better safe than sorry" approach. This book will give you the tools to implement this approach and we hope you will feel empowered by your position and ability to change the trajectory of what could be a chronic and debilitating illness.

REFERENCES

Addington, J., Cadenhead, K. S., Cornblatt, B. A., Mathalon, D. H., McGlashan, T. H., Perkins, D. O.,...Cannon, T. D. (2012). North American Prodrome Longitudinal Study (NAPLS 2): Overview and recruitment. *Schizophrenia Research, 142*(1–3), 77–82. doi: 10.1016/j.schres.2012.09.012

Addington, J., Piskulic, D., & Marshall, C. (2010). Psychosocial treatments for schizophrenia. *Current Directions in Psychological Science, 19*(4), 260–263. doi:10.1177/0963721410377743

Addington, J., Stowkowy, J., Cadenhead, K. S., Cornblatt, B. A., McGlashan, T. H., Perkins, D. O.,...Cannon, T. D. (2013). Early traumatic experiences in those at clinical high risk for psychosis. *Early Intervention in Psychiatry, 7*(3), 300–305. doi:10.1111/eip.12020

Amador, X. F., & David, A. S. (2004). *Insight and psychosis.* Oxford, England: Oxford University Press.

American Psychiatric Association. (2013). *Diagnostic and statistical manual of mental disorders* (5th ed.). Arlington, VA: American Psychiatric Publishing.

Bechdolf, A., Thompson, A., Nelson, B., Cotton, S., Simmons, M. B., Amminger, G. P.,...Yung, A. R. (2010). Experience of trauma and conversion to psychosis in an ultra-high-risk (prodromal) group. *Acta Psychiatrica Scandinavica, 121*(5), 377–384. doi:10.1111/j.1600–0447.2010.01542

Brabban, A., & Turkington, D. (2002). The search for meaning: Detecting congruence between life events, underlying schema and psychotic symptoms—formulation-driven and schema-focused cognitive behavioural therapy for a neuroleptic-resistant schizophrenic patient with a delusional memory. In A. P. Morrison (Ed.), *Casebook of cognitive therapy for psychosis* (pp. 59–75). New York, NY: Brunner-Routledge.

Cardno, A. G., & Owen, M. J. (2014). Genetic relationships between schizophrenia, bipolar disorder, and schizoaffective disorder. *Schizophrenia Bulletin, 40*(3), 504–515.

Carpenter, W. T., & Davis, J. M. (2012). Another view of the history of antipsychotic drug discovery and development. *Molecular Psychiatry, 17*, 1168–1173.

Cella, M., Huddy, V., Reeder, C., & Wykes, T. (2012). Cognitive remediation therapy for schizophrenia. *Minerva Psichiatrica, 53*(3), 185–196.

Centers for Disease Control and Prevention. (2013, October 4). *Burden of mental illness.* Retrieved from http://www.cdc.gov/mentalhealth/basics/burden.htm

Craddock, N., O'Donovan, M. C., & Owen, M. J. (2009). Psychosis genetics: Modeling the relationship between schizophrenia, bipolar disorder, and mixed (or "schizoaffective") psychosis. *Schizophrenia Bulletin, 35*(3), 482–490.

Cross-Disorder Group of the Psychiatric Genomics Consortium. (2013). Genetic relationship between five psychiatric disorders estimated from genome-wide SNPs. *Nature Genetics, 45*(9), 984–994.

Falconer, D. S. (1965). The inheritance of liability to certain diseases, estimated from the incidence among relatives. *Annals of Human Genetics, 29*(1), 51–76.

Fowles, D. C. (1992). Schizophrenia: Diathesis-stress revisited. *Annual Review of Psychology, 43,* 303–336.

Gottesman, I. I., & Shields, J. (1967). A polygenic theory of schizophrenia. *Genetics, 58,* 199–205.

Hamm, J. A., Hasson-Ohayon, I., Kukla, M., & Lysaker, P. H. (2013). Individual psychotherapy for schizophrenia: Trends and developments in the wake of the recovery movement. *Psychology Research & Behavior Management, 6,* 45–53. doi:10.2147/PRBM.S47891

Hogarty, G. E., & Flesher, S. (1999). Practice principles of cognitive enhancement therapy for schizophrenia. *Schizophrenia Bulletin, 25*(4), 693–708.

Hongyun, Q., Jie, Z., Zhenping, W., Haiying, M., Caiying, Y., Fuzhen, C.,…Ming, Z. (2014). Duration of untreated psychosis and clinical outcomes of first-episode schizophrenia: A 4-year follow-up study. *Shanghai Archives of Psychiatry, 26*(1), 42–48. doi:10.3969/j.issn.1002–0829.2014.01.006

Insel, T. R. (2008). Assessing the economic costs of serious mental illness. *The American Journal of Psychiatry, 165*(6), 663–665.

Kopelowicz, A., Liberman, R. P., & Wallace, C. J. (2003). Psychiatric rehabilitation for schizophrenia. *International Journal of Psychology and Psychological Therapy, 3*(2), 283–298.

Kurtz, M. M., & Mueser, K. T. (2008). A meta-analysis of controlled research on social skills training for schizophrenia. *Journal of Consulting and Clinical Psychology, 76*(3), 491–504. doi:10.1037/0022–006X.76.3.491

Lehman, A. F., Kreyenbuhl, J., Buchanan, R. W., Dickerson, F. B., Dixon, L. B., Goldberg, R.,…Steinwachs, D. M. (2004). The Schizophrenia Patient Outcomes Research Team (PORT): Updated treatment recommendations 2003. *Schizophrenia Bulletin, 30,* 193–217.

Leichsenring, F., & Leibing, E. (2007). Psychodynamic psychotherapy: A systematic review of techniques, indications and empirical evidence. *Psychology and Psychotherapy, 80*(Pt. 2), 217–228.

Lockwood, C., Page, T., & Conroy-Hiller, T. (2004). Effectiveness of individual therapy and group therapy in the treatment of schizophrenia. *JBI Library of Systematic Reviews, 2*(2), 60–103.

Mantt, C., Eng, C., Pokinko, M., Ryan, R. T., Torres-Berrio, A., Lopez, J. P.,…Fores, C. (2013). *dcc* orchestrates the development of the prefrontal cortex during adolescence and is altered in psychiatric patients. *Translational Psychiatry, 3*(e338), 1–13. doi:10.1038/tp.2013.105

McGorry, P. D., Edwards, J., Mihalopoulos, C., Harrigan, S. M., & Jackson, H. J. (1996). EPPIC: An evolving system of early detection and optimal management. *Schizophrenia Bulletin, 22*(2), 305–326. doi: 10.1093/schbul/22.2.305

McRenolds, D., Mehta, P., & Nasrallah, H. A. (2013). Evaluation and treatment strategies in patients with schizophrenia and comorbid depression. *Psychiatric Annals, 43*(10), 446–453.

Morrison, A. K. (2009). Cognitive behavior therapy for people with schizophrenia. *Psychiatry (Edgmont), 6*(12), 32–39.

Mueser, K. T., Deavers, F., Penn, D. L., & Cassisi, J. E. (2013). Psychosocial treatments for schizophrenia. *Annual Review of Clinical Psychology, 9,* 465–497. doi: 10.1146/annurev-clinpsy-050212-185620

National Alliance on Mental Illness. (2015, January 19). *Mental health conditions.* Retrieved from http://www.nami.org

National Institute of Mental Health. (2009). *Schizophrenia.* Bethesda, MD: Author.

Pilling, S., Bebbington, P., Kuipers, E., Garety, P., Geddes, J., Orbach, G., & Morgan, C. (2002). Psychological treatments in schizophrenia: I. Meta-analysis of family intervention and cognitive behaviour therapy. *Psychological Medicine, 32,* 763–782.

Rathod, S., Kingdon, D., Weiden, P., & Turkington, D. (2008). Cognitive-behavioral therapy for medication-resistant schizophrenia: A review. *Journal of Psychiatric Practice, 14*(1), 22–33.

Ruhrmann, S., Schultze-Lutter, F., Salokangas, R. K., Heinimaa, M., Linszen, D., Dingemans, P., ... Klosterkotter, J. (2010). Prediction of psychosis in adolescents and young adults at high risk: Results from the prospective European Prediction of Psychosis Study. *Archives of General Psychiatry, 67*(3), 241–251. doi:10.1001/archgenpsychiatry.2009.206

Sturman, D. A., & Moghaddam, B. (2011). The neurobiology of adolescence: Changes in brain architecture, functional dynamics, and behavioral tendencies. *Neuroscience and Biobehavioral Reviews, 35*(8), 1704–1712.

Thompson, A. D., Nelson, B., Yuen, H. P., Lin, A., Amminger, G. P., McGorry, P. D., ... Yung, A. R. (2014). Sexual trauma increases the risk of developing psychosis in an ultra high-risk "prodromal" population. *Schizophrenia Bulletin, 40*(3), 697–706. doi:10.1093/schbul/sbt032

Tsuang, M. T., Stone, W. S., Tarbox, S. I., & Faraone, S. V. (2002). An integration of schizophrenia with schizotypy: Identification of schizotaxia and implications for research on treatment and prevention. *Schizophrenia Research, 54*(1–2), 169–175.

Van Winkel, R., Van Nierop, M., Myin-Germeys, I., & Van Os, J. (2013). Childhood trauma as a cause of psychosis: Linking genes, psychology, and biology. *Canadian Journal of Psychiatry*, 58(1), 44–51.

World Health Organization. (2003). *Investing in mental health.* Geneva, Switzerland: Department of Mental Health and Substance Dependence, Noncommunicable Diseases and Mental Health, and World Health Organization.

CHAPTER **TWO**

What Does a First Psychotic Episode Look Like?

This chapter aims to introduce the different symptoms characteristic of a psychotic episode. We expect that some of these may be familiar to you through your own experience or knowledge, and that others may be unfamiliar presentations of familiar symptoms. As we discussed in Chapter 1, a psychotic episode can include one, some, or all of the symptoms that are discussed here. We hope to show that these symptoms can present in different ways at different times within a person, and across individuals when comparing symptomatic individuals to one another. Although "diagnosis" is not the goal of this book, we believe that some knowledge of these symptoms is helpful when assisting in a crisis to better understand what is being experienced and perceived by the individual in the early throws of a psychotic episode. It is important to note that the following symptoms are experienced as real and genuine. Over time, they can become unquestioned truths, and those who believe otherwise are perceived as misguided and perhaps untrustworthy.

There are five major categories of symptoms discussed in this chapter: positive symptoms, negative symptoms, disorganized symptoms, affective symptoms, and cognitive symptoms. See Table 2.1 for abbreviated definitions and examples of these symptoms for reference. In addition, there are two associated symptom categories that are important: abnormal motor behavior and level of insight. An identified *psychotic episode* will have symptoms from the positive symptom category, in addition to one or more of the other categories. As discussed in the section "What

TABLE 2.1

Symptoms of a Psychotic Episode

Symptoms	Definition	Example
Positive	Symptoms that are *in addition to* or *added* to typical experience	– Hearing voices or sounds – Seeing forms, figures, or shadows
Negative	Symptoms that are *absent* or *less than* typical experience	– Low motivation – Decreased pleasure – Isolation – Decreased emotional expression – Decreased speech
Disorganized	Thought and behavior patterns that impair organization and logic abilities	– Tangential speech – Word salad – Wearing a parka in the heat of summer
Affective	Subjective and objective mood states	– Depression – Mania – Anxiety
Cognitive	Impaired thinking abilities that are noted deviations from prior abilities	– Memory problems – Attention problems – Comprehension problems
Motor behavior	Abnormal motor movements	– Tics
Lack of insight	Level of awareness of symptoms and illness	– Limited awareness of functional decline – Limited reality-testing abilities

Are Psychotic Disorders?" in Chapter 1, different symptom combinations as well as other factors such as number, severity, duration of symptoms, and impact on functioning determine diagnoses such as schizophrenia, schizoaffective disorder, or bipolar disorder. However, as diagnosis is not our aim for this text and understanding the "how much, how bad, and how long" is not as important here, we focus instead on the qualities and presentation of such conditions.

For many young adults with psychosis, the symptoms discussed in the following will develop or become more elaborate or intrusive over time. For some, the process can be so gradual that the symptoms progress slowly without much notice. For others, the introduction of symptoms can be sudden, shocking, and scary.

FIVE MAJOR CATEGORIES OF SYMPTOMS ASSOCIATED WITH A PSYCHOTIC EPISODE

Positive Symptoms

Positive symptoms of psychosis refer to those symptoms that are *added* to previous functioning, and *additions* to the typical experience of most people. That is, these are experiences that the person did not experience before the onset of psychosis but are now present. Positive symptoms of psychosis include delusions and hallucinations.

DELUSIONS

Delusions are fixed beliefs that do not change in the face of conflicting evidence. Delusions may or may not be *bizarre* in nature; they are deemed bizarre if they are implausible or strange in quality. For example, someone experiencing bizarre delusions may believe that celebrities are able to read his or her thoughts and use their movies to respond to them, or that the individual has been chosen as the leader of an alien kingdom. There is a clear implausibility to this scenario, which helps us to identify it as bizarre. A nonbizarre delusion, on the other hand, may seem possible even if unlikely. For instance, someone may believe that a teacher is plotting against him or her and communicating taunting messages during lectures. Although this seems highly unlikely, it is indeed possible that such a situation could occur. For many individuals who experience delusions, their delusions maintain a consistent "theme," that is, they experience a similarity in the content of delusions over time. However, some individuals may have less consistent thought patterns where delusions seem to come and go, or alter significantly in different situations.

Delusional thought can be related to nearly any subject; however, some themes tend to occur more frequently. Some more frequently occurring themes of delusions include persecutory delusions, erotomanic delusions, grandiose delusions, and somatic delusions. Individuals who experience *persecutory delusions* believe that they are being wronged by others. They may believe that people are sabotaging them, planning to harm or harass them, or monitoring them in some way. For instance, individuals experiencing persecutory delusions may believe that their food is being poisoned, that coworkers are plotting to have them fired when they are not, that neighbors are monitoring their behavior in order to exploit them later, or that someone is trying to kill them for some gain. Take the following example:

> Jill was starting to get the sense that her mother was angry with her. Her mother's normal requests, such as cleaning her room or finishing her homework, began to feel threatening. Jill began to notice her mother's detailed approach to making dinner and wondered if there was a reason for such detail—if she was putting poisonous particles in her food. Jill very carefully watched her family members eat their meals and felt that her mother was watching her, specifically, as she approached her plate. To be safe, Jill began to request only pre-packaged, individually wrapped foods and would not eat anything in the house with a broken seal.

Erotomanic delusions are typified by romantic or sexual preoccupations in which the individuals may inaccurately believe that another person is in love with them, or that they have a romantic or sexual relationship with someone they do not. A person may believe that he or she has a romantic relationship with a famous figure, or the person may believe that a neighbor is in love with him or her when it is not the case. This may sound familiar to you as there have been cases where celebrity or political figures have encountered individuals who very strongly believed that they were in a very intimate relationship with the famous figure. *Grandiose delusions* are those in which individuals believe themselves to be important, famous, or wealthy when they are not. For example, individuals with grandiose delusions may believe that they have a responsibility to save the world from a disaster, that they are heir to a fortune, have the ability to read others' minds and control their behaviors, or that they are a prominent religious figure. For example, it is not uncommon for individuals with a grandiose delusion to assert that they own the psychiatric hospital into which they have been recently admitted. *Somatic delusions* are delusions focused on one's body or health. An individual experiencing a somatic delusion may believe that he or she has a deadly disease, is pregnant, or needs an organ transplant. These, of course, can only be considered delusions when medical evidence has ruled out such possibilities.

For some people experiencing delusions, their beliefs may be pleasant or reassuring to them; for example, if some individuals experience a delusion that they have millions of dollars, they may find that belief exciting. Or, if they believe themselves to have a special religious purpose, this may be comforting and empowering, rather than distressing. Conversely, individuals may find the content of their delusions distressing if, for instance, they believe that they are going to be harmed in some way (e.g., killed by their family). Regardless of whether delusions are distressing or helpful, acting in accordance with them may result in notable consequences in an individual's life. Consider how some people might behave if they genuinely believed their life was being threatened by a neighbor. They may become hypervigilant, watching the neighbor's movements to ensure that they were not coming after them. They may become irritable or even accusatory in interactions with the neighbor. They may misinterpret neutral events as threatening. Consider the following example.

> Lyle took his usual seat in the cafeteria and unwrapped his sandwich. He noticed that the new girl, who had just been transferred, was standing at the door looking around the cafeteria. She approached the otherwise empty table where Lyle was sitting. "Can I sit here?" she asked. Lyle shrugged and continued eating his sandwich. "Thanks!" she said, and smiled at him. Lyle avoided eye contact. Of all the tables in the cafeteria, why would she choose his? What was she trying to do? She was clearly up to something, Lyle just needed to figure out what before it was too late.

Conversely, imagine how individuals may react if they believe they are a religious deity with a duty to save the population from an outside threat. They may try to spread their message and discuss their important position to ease pain and fear in others. They may appear to plan elaborate interventions and protectants, or feel that they need to sacrifice themselves for the greater good. Outwardly, these behaviors would seem odd, irrational, and unreasonable; however, when we consider that the individual truly believes these circumstances to be true, the behaviors seem more understandable. This, of course, is why knowledge of these symptoms becomes important. Empathizing with an individual's experience and perspective of his or her symptoms becomes crucial when introducing and initiating help. These strategies are discussed at length in the next chapter.

HALLUCINATIONS

Hallucinations are the perceptual experiences that occur in the absence of an external stimulus. Hallucinations often feel so real that a person may not be able to identify that the experience is internal and not caused by something external. The vividness with which you are reading these words at this moment is the same experience or "realness" that a person with hallucinations perceives his or her experience.

Hallucinations can occur in any of the five sensory modalities: auditory (hearing), visual (sight), gustatory (taste), olfactory (smell), or tactile (touch). *Auditory hallucinations* are the most commonly experienced in schizophrenia. Many individuals who experience auditory hallucinations hear clear, intelligible voices that may comment on their behavior, communicate information, or command them to engage in certain behaviors. Some people who experience psychosis may hear the voice of someone they know, while others may not identify voices as familiar. Some may experience auditory hallucinations that are not voices, but other sounds such as music, static, or beeping. Some people may identify these sounds or voices as originating from outside of themselves, while others may feel that the stimuli are produced internally. Even if a person is able to identify that the voices or sounds are coming from an internal source, he or she is often not able to identify this as a symptom or psychiatric concern but instead identify another explanation for this experience. A portion of young people with psychosis experience *command hallucinations*, where the content of the hallucination encourages or demands that the individual behave in some way. The commands may be innocuous, such as "go eat lunch now" or "put down the book"; however, in some cases, commands can encourage risky behavior (e.g., committing a crime or running into the street), or instruct harm to oneself or others. As mentioned previously, the symptoms can develop over time such as that in the following example:

> At the age of 17, Sam began hearing unintelligible whispers. They occurred outside of his head and could be heard with both ears. At first, he couldn't recognize any detail about them, but over the course of several months he was able to identify a man's voice and a woman's voice. The woman's voice commented on his daily activities, such as running commentary about his behaviors. The man's voice, on the other hand, was negative. It started by making negative judgments about others (e.g., "He's a bad person and he's going to hurt you") and later became more intense and personal (e.g., "No one likes you; you should kill yourself. Grab that knife!").

Visual hallucinations refer to the experience of seeing something that is not present. Often, the content of visual hallucinations is not as well defined as that of auditory hallucinations. For instance, individuals may report seeing human figures with little detail, or seeing a tree change shape. Some individuals who experience visual phenomena report that they experience poorly defined figures or objects, as opposed to well-defined or realistic images. However, it is possible to see fully formed and detailed visions. The visual themes can be any number of things; they could be religious in nature such as angel figures or the head of a devil, self-reflections such as seeing one's face morph into another image, or more abstract and unrealistic combinations such as an animal with a cow's body and a cat's head. Unfortunately, many visual hallucinations are scary and are perceived as threatening in some way.

People who experience *gustatory hallucinations* may report lingering tastes in their mouth, tastes that come and go intensely, or feeling that the taste of their food is not what is expected. Similarly, *olfactory hallucinations* may be lingering or discrete with intense smells. Often gustatory and olfactory hallucinations are not pleasant in content, that is, an individual is unlikely to experience hallucination of the taste and smell of chocolate cake. Rather, unpleasant sensations such as the taste and smell of blood or metal appear to be more likely. *Tactile hallucinations* are sensations of touch, and may include feeling tickled, poked, or held down. They may also include sensations of some object or animal crawling on them such as spiders or snakes.

People with hallucinations often experience an overwhelming number of stimuli at any given time. Many of us experience a feeling of over-stimulation on a daily basis as we try to multitask our way through our day. However, the experience of a young person with psychosis is often even more overwhelming. Imagine that you are trying to have an important conversation with your boss, but at the same time the fire alarm is sounding, your mother is on the phone telling you step by step how to bake her famous green bean casserole, and there is a movie you have been wanting to see playing behind your boss's head. Would you be able to concentrate on the conversation? How effectively would you be able to express your feelings or concerns to your boss? How long could you continue the conversation? Imagine if you also had an underlying fear that someone may be breaking into your home to steal the new television you just bought, or that you feared that your mother, on the phone, might be trying to convey some hidden message within her casserole recipe. For individuals who experience psychotic symptoms, this experience is not as unrealistic as it sounds; they frequently, and for some people constantly, experience overstimulation that reaches this level. It is not difficult to see how challenging it would be to engage in daily activities with this amount of stimulation.

While you may encounter someone who is currently overwhelmed by a similar psychotic scenario, you may also encounter an individual who is simply trying to manage one of these experiences. Discerning between the two could be a difficult task. Luckily, that is not something we believe you will need to do because *distress* looks pretty universal no matter the cause. In the section "How Do Symptoms Appear in Daily Life?" of this chapter and in the following chapters we discuss more about the presentation of *distress* in adolescents and young adults experiencing a psychotic episode and how to support them in receiving assistance.

Negative Symptoms

Negative symptoms represent things that have been taken away from an individual's previous functioning, and reflect *absences* from the typical experience of most people. They are aspects of functioning that an individual once had, but have decreased or are no longer present after the onset of the illness. Negative symptoms are often some of the first symptoms to emerge in a psychotic illness, and they often present before positive symptoms. However, you will likely notice that they mirror what seems like normal and expected variations in adolescence and young adulthood. Although parents, teachers, and friends usually notice them, they often persist for some time before they are identified as areas of concern because, in the short term, they may seem typical adolescent behavior. Negative symptoms associated with psychosis can be thought of as the five A's: flat Affect (diminished emotional expression), Avolition, Alogia, Anhedonia, and Asociality.

Individuals who experience *flat affect* (diminished emotional expression) may exhibit an absence of facial expression despite reporting that they feel emotions. In interactions with individuals experiencing this symptom, it may be difficult to tell whether they are interested or engaged in the conversation. They may offer little feedback in terms of facial expression, and demonstrate little to no range in their emotional expressions. Additionally, people with this negative symptom may make less frequent eye contact, or speak in a monotone manner with little inflection. However, this is not necessarily related to how they actually feel. Individuals exhibiting flat affect can and do experience very strong emotions of all types, but they may not be in line with their outward emotional expression. Unfortunately, some people with psychosis do report feeling "numb" at times, and thus may have more congruence between their inner experience and outward expression.

Avolition refers to a decrease in self-initiated activities and low motivation. Individuals may not make independent decisions to engage in activities, showing little interest in obligations or recreation. They may report substantial difficulty motivating themselves to attend school or work, or to meet basic hygiene needs. They may have difficulty identifying a preference for various activities, and instead spend significant amounts of time engaged in passive activities such as watching TV. It is important to differentiate avolition from laziness. For people who experience avolition, even seemingly routine daily tasks might take what feels like tremendous effort. They may avoid completing tasks or engaging in activities in order to avoid feelings of physical or emotional fatigue. It is important to consider this as a symptom, as opposed to oppositionality or "laziness," which may be normative for some young adults.

Consider the following example of changes in behavior and how this may be a sign of a significant problem.

> Tenielle's mother noticed that she was not keeping up herself like she used to. Over the course of the past 6 months, her once fashion-conscious daughter was now donning sweatpants to school and reported "not really caring" about what she wore.

Individuals who experience *alogia* will demonstrate a reduction in speech and communicative abilities. Compared with previous behavior, they may speak only when directly addressed, but rarely produce spontaneous speech or begin a conversation. Some individuals may also experience *thought blocking*, in which the person may appear to lose their train of thought in the middle of a sentence. They may abruptly stop speaking without acknowledging that they were just speaking, or demonstrate a prolonged delay in response. For instance, when asked a question or spoken to, there may be a several-second delay before the person is able to respond. Some individuals may also have a limited repertoire of responses. For instance, they may respond to nearly any question with "yes," "no," or "I don't know" with little variability. Together, these experiences often contribute to substantial difficulty in communicating.

Anhedonia refers to an individual's reduced ability to experience pleasure, even in situations that the person used to enjoy. Individuals may decline to participate in activities they previously sought out, such as withdrawing from athletic, academic, occupational, and social activities. For example, someone who was devoted to music and played in a band might begin to express that he or she no longer wants to be a part of the band because playing just "isn't fun anymore." This symptom becomes most apparent when individuals begin to decrease participation in activities that were once an important part of their daily life and routine.

Finally, *asociality* refers to an apparent lack of interest in social relationships. Individuals may express preferring to be alone, or feeling uncomfortable in social situations, even if they enjoyed them before symptom onset. Some people experiencing psychosis will stop spending time or making plans with friends entirely. Solitary activities such as watching TV or playing video games often become much more prominent.

Unfortunately, individuals with negative symptoms often experience more than one of these symptoms. Consider the following example:

> Shawn recently began seeing a psychiatrist after beginning to feel that someone was watching him in his home through cameras hidden in the walls. Shawn told the psychiatrist that he also noticed a small scratch on his forearm and was beginning to wonder if a monitoring device had been implanted while he was asleep. His mother couldn't see the scratch, but he insisted it was there! The psychiatrist inquired about the months leading up to this period of concern and learned that Shawn has become more withdrawn. He was still attending school daily but the work was feeling more difficult than normal. Even literature, his favorite subject, was becoming more daunting. Shawn had also stopped hanging out with his friends because it "takes too much work, I feel too tired." The psychiatrist also noted that Shawn was expressionless during his discussion of these changes in his life, despite saying that he was confused by them and felt lonely.

When taken together, these symptoms sound similar to depression, which is discussed in the "Affective Symptoms" section of this chapter. The hallmark of depression is sadness and negative symptoms can occur outside of feeling sad. Moreover, there are a number of other symptoms that need to be present before depression can be identified as the cause.

Disorganized Symptoms

When you initially hear the term "disorganization" you may be thinking about tidiness, and organization in a typical form. However, in reference to psychosis, disorganization has a much broader reach. Young adults who experience *disorganization* are likely to manifest these symptoms in a variety of modalities. This may include *disorganized thought* patterns in which they are unable to maintain a linear thought. That is, they may have difficulty connecting thoughts in a logical way. Largely, disorganized thought patterns are most evident in a person's speech when interacting with others. The person may have difficulty telling a story or relaying the day's events in a way that can be easily followed. This is not simply "being scattered" but rather the person may seem to easily be taken off topic and have difficulty reorienting to what he or she was previously discussing. This may be evidenced by *derailment*, the switching of topics without an identifiable link, or *loose associations* in which the person seems to link topics based on superficial or loosely related aspects. For instance, an example of a loose association might be: "My brother used to play football, but he just didn't put his heart into it. If your heart stops beating you die or you'll be heartbroken." In this example, the individual loosely associated the metaphorical meaning of "heart" to the physical, and then a different type of metaphor. Another indication of disorganized thought patterns is *tangentiality*. Those experiencing psychosis may demonstrate tangentiality by diverting a conversation to a topic that is related to what they are discussing; however, they may be unable to redirect their thought process to return to the point. Consider the following example:

> I've been doing well in classes. Even my math class! I was never very good at math even though I had an excellent teacher in second grade. That was a tough year since it was also when my parents got divorced and they were fighting all the time. I still won the science fair that year though, and went on vacation with my friend and his family. I did a lot of really fun things in second grade.

In this example, the person has diverted the conversation on to a tangent, which is not uncommon in everyday conversation. However, for individuals experiencing disorganized thought, they may not be able to recognize that they have diverted from the original subject, and may not be able to trace back the steps of the conversation to determine how they arrived at the current topic. In rare circumstances, thought and speech may become so disorganized that there is little to no connection between the words being spoken. This phenomenon is known as *word salad* or *incoherence*. When word salad is present, it is often spoken with the inflection of a coherent sentence; however, the words are unrelated and grammatically nonsensical.

Individuals who experience disorganized thought may also exhibit disorganization in their *behavior*. Young adults whose behavior is disorganized may present as having difficulty focusing on one task at a time. They may lose their train of thought during one task and quickly move to another. Disorganization may present behaviorally as forgetfulness. For example, a person who has an appointment may lose his or her appointment card each week, and despite stating that he or she will put it in a wallet "where he or she won't lose it" it seems to go missing. In some cases, disorganized thought and behavior patterns interfere with a person's ability to meet basic daily needs, as his or her mind is not able to organize and prioritize tasks in a typical fashion. For example, individuals may have difficulty with hygiene. This can result in a disheveled and malodorous appearance. Disorganization may also lead to impairment in judgment, as the person may have an inability to realistically and logically think through potential consequences of his or her actions. For instance, an individual may leave the house dressed in summer clothing on a cold winter day without having considered that he or she will likely be uncomfortably cold or be vulnerable to illness. Similarly, he or she may have difficulty in organizing plans for future behavior. An individual may be able to identify a future goal (i.e., becoming a lawyer), but be unable to identify the most basic steps that would need to be achieved in order to begin pursuing such a goal. Planning for the more immediate future may also be impaired. For example, someone may have difficulty organizing a schedule of activities for the following day in a realistic manner. Table 2.1 provides a summary of the symptoms of psychosis for your reference.

Affective Symptoms

Some young people who experience psychosis may also experience disturbances in mood referred to as *affective symptoms*. *Affect* refers to the subjective report of how someone is *feeling*, as well as observable aspects of mood. Observable aspects may include facial expression, verbal tone and rate, motor behavior, engagement in activities, and thought content and process. These symptoms describe a variety of ways in which a person's behavior might change in accordance with his or her mood. It is important to note that affective symptoms alone do not indicate the presence of psychosis; rather, they may co-occur and interact with symptoms of psychosis. The mood states discussed in the following are not an exhaustive list, but rather the most common affective experiences associated with a psychotic episode in adolescents and young adults.

DEPRESSION
Young adults experiencing psychosis may also experience symptoms of depression. Symptoms of depression include changes in sleep or eating patterns, loss of interest in previously enjoyed activities, low energy,

feelings of worthlessness or hopelessness, difficulty with thinking or concentration, irritability, subjective feeling of depression, and suicidal ideation. It may be particularly difficult to differentiate symptoms of depression from negative symptoms of psychosis as they may appear outwardly similar in many instances. However, this differentiation is often only of concern to mental health professionals who are determining a diagnosis. When considering a supportive interaction with the individual, such differentiation is less important. A mnemonic that is often used to remember the symptoms of depression is SIG E CAPS (Caplan & Stern, 2008) and is outlined in Table 2.2.

Depressive symptoms can occur as a reaction to psychotic symptoms such as in response to voices making disparaging remarks, or indirectly such as in response to realization of managing a lifelong illness. The latter response is common across chronic medical conditions. In addition, depression can occur somewhat independently and not directly related to psychotic illness. Depression may also be present before the onset of any psychotic symptoms and may have developed for a number of different reasons. In this case, depression usually exacerbates symptoms of psychosis.

For individuals experiencing psychosis, it is important to consider the manner in which psychotic symptoms may interact with symptoms of depression. This may most notably be seen in the form of mood-congruent hallucinations, which refers to hallucinations with content that matches the person's mood symptoms at the time. For example, if someone is experiencing depression, this may include the experience of voices

TABLE 2.2
Symptoms of Depression: SIG E CAPS

Sleep changes: either an increase or decrease in sleep
Interest (loss): loss of interest in activities that used to be of interest
Guilt: feeling poorly about oneself
Energy (loss of): feeling fatigued or having difficulty motivating one self
Concentration: difficulty concentrating
Appetite changes: either an increased or decreased appetite
Psychomotor (movement) changes: either appearing fidgety and constantly moving, or lethargic with slowed movements
Suicidal thoughts or preoccupation with death

saying deprecating statements ("You are a terrible person," "Everyone hates you," or "They're talking about how pathetic you are"). Or, if a person experiences mood-congruent hallucinations during mania, he or she may include grandiose content or content encouraging impulsivity ("You are special and people need to appreciate that," "Just run up on stage, everyone will want to see you!" "She is into you, she's just pretending not to be, so go ahead and kiss her"). Even more concerning is hallucinatory content that may relate to suicidal ideation. This hallucinatory content may encourage thoughts about suicide, reinforce hopelessness, or even command a person to end his or her life ("Everyone would be happier if you were dead," "No one would miss you," "Take that knife and do it"). Imagine the following:

> Think of your best friend, or someone you care very much about. Now, this person is joined by a new coworker and they work together all day, every day. The coworker turns to this person throughout the day saying horrible things like "You're a loser, no one loves you," "The world would be better if you were dead." This new coworker waits for your friend to make a mistake and whispers "Oh, you screwed up again. You should just give up and kill yourself. You can't do anything right." How do you imagine your friend is feeling after several days of this? How long could your friend hear these things before he or she begins to believe them?

This is not dissimilar to the experience of individuals who have this type of hallucinatory content. Recall that hallucinations appear to the individuals as true experiences in their reality. Imagine the emotional toll that would be taken on individuals who heard these terrible things said to them constantly, particularly if they are already feeling sad and depressed.

MANIA

In the way that depression is characterized by low mood, mania is a condition that results from mood being too high. *Mania* refers to a period of time in which an individual experiences expansive or elevated mood, or irritability, and excessive energy. A person experiencing manic symptoms may appear euphoric, happy, excited, or irritable without identifiable reason. There are a number of factors that differentiate mania from a normal state of being "in a good or bad mood."

For instance, mania may result in a number of changes in the way a person communicates with others. An individual may evidence *pressured speech* in which a person may speak for an unusual length of time without pauses, often with an increased speed of speech. It may be difficult to interject or direct the topics of conversation, and efforts to do so may seem to irritate the person. Further complicating communication is the experience of *flight of ideas*, or the experience that thoughts are racing, occurring several at a time, or with a frequency that makes it difficult to communicate them coherently. It is likely challenging to engage in a conversation with someone experiencing mania. Conversation is often one-sided and hard to follow. This may be particularly true if an individual is experiencing symptoms of psychosis while also experiencing an episode of mania.

A person experiencing mania is also likely to demonstrate a number of changes in behavior due to the increase in energy that occurs. For instance, during a manic episode, individuals are likely to exhibit a decreased need for sleep; they may sleep only a few hours nightly and wake feeling rested and full of energy. Time usually spent sleeping may be replaced with *increased goal-directed behavior*. This refers to the tendency of individuals experiencing mania to engage in many different activities and pursue new, lofty, and usually unrealistic goals. For instance, a young person experiencing mania may start a new business, develop several new hobbies, connect socially with a new group of people, decide to move, apply to several colleges, and commit to a volunteering obligation all in the same week. Individuals may begin a number of new projects, but may be unlikely to complete any of them due to *distractibility*. During an episode of mania, people are easily distracted, moving quickly from one activity to the next leaving many things unfinished. This is likely to make it difficult for individuals to function in their typical roles. For instance, a person employed in an office may have difficulty adhering to his or her regular work schedule due to other undertakings. Instead of following the supervisor's directions, an individual may leave primary tasks incomplete but may begin extraneous tasks such as rearranging the furniture in the office and organizing an office potluck. It is easy to imagine that this person could be in danger of losing his or her job if these behaviors persist.

Furthermore, during an episode of mania individuals may evidence inflated self-esteem or *grandiosity*. They may present themselves with an air of entitlement and an implication that others should respond to them with deference and admiration. They may respond defensively to implications that they are imperfect or possess some weakness. For instance, they may insult or otherwise devalue someone who points out the unrealistic nature of their ideas. In addition, some individuals may demonstrate questionable judgment and impulsivity. They may engage in behaviors that have potentially serious consequences without any forethought or consideration of ramifications. For example, a young person experiencing mania may engage in excessive spending or gambling and accumulate substantial debt, engage in risky sexual behavior by having unprotected sex with multiple partners, or experiment with drugs. All of these behaviors have potentially serious consequences; however, when someone experiences mania, he or she may impulsively engage in these or other risky behaviors without regard for future consequences. It is also important to differentiate these behaviors from typical adolescent experimentation. Rather than curiosity, mania may contribute to feelings of invincibility.

For individuals who experience symptoms of mania and psychosis at the same time, the interaction between these symptom clusters can become problematic. Consider the following example of how these interactions may manifest:

> Kelsey has a delusional belief that the stars of her favorite television show are communicating with her through dialogue on the program. No matter how many times her family and friends tell her this is not true, she believes it. Recently, Kelsey has also begun to experience symptoms of mania. She has begun writing several letters and e-mails daily to the show's stars; however, she is unsatisfied that they haven't responded in writing yet. She stays up all night watching reruns of the show to see if she can figure out why the stars haven't responded to her. Today, she decided that she will fly to Los Angeles to talk with them in person about the messages they have been sending her. She is planning to sell her car to pay for the trip.

In this example, we can see that Kelsey's ability to act on her delusional beliefs is fueled by the impulsivity, increased energy, and irresponsibility associated with mania. For individuals who experience both psychotic and manic symptoms, this interaction is common. That is, mania facilitates the person being able to follow through with action based on delusional beliefs or other psychotic phenomena. An easy mnemonic for manic symptoms is DIG FAST (Caplan & Stern, 2008) and is elaborated on in Table 2.3.

ANXIETY

Similar to depression and mania, anxiety is also commonly associated with psychosis. Anxiety symptoms of psychosis may include a fear of being followed or monitored or receiving constant negative feedback from voices about one's behavior or thoughts. Although it is entirely

TABLE 2.3
Symptoms of Mania: DIG FAST

Distractibility: reduced concentration, difficulty completing tasks
Irresponsibility: engaging in risky behaviors without regard for consequences
Grandiosity: belief that one is overly important or superior to others
Flight of ideas: rapidly shifting ideas with little or no connection among them
Activity: increase in goal-directed behaviors
Sleep: reduced need for sleep
Talkativeness: excessive talking with pressured speech

possible that someone may have suffered from significant anxiety before the development of a psychotic episode, any new or lingering anxiety is likely to be related to or intertwined with psychotic content. Because the majority of positive symptoms include negative content, there is much to be worried or fearful about. For example, if a young adult hears voices that are commenting on his or her behavior and making judgments about actions or choices, it may be expected that anxiety about making choices and reactions will develop or heighten. Moreover, auditory and visual hallucinations may be constant, only present in response to certain stimuli, or be present in unpredictable patterns. Concern about the return of symptoms may also contribute to anxiety. Finally, persecutory delusions are particularly associated with anxiety, as concern about being targeted, threatened, or monitored is likely to induce worry and fear. Panic attacks, a severe state of physiological anxiety, can also occur.

Cognitive Symptoms

Cognitive decline is a common symptom of psychosis, particularly with chronic psychosis. In addition to negative symptoms, cognitive symptoms are some of the first to appear and are often part of the initial cluster of changes that signal concern. Because school is often the primary role of an adolescent or young adult, changes in areas of cognitive functioning become noticeable by parents and teachers even before the full onset of psychotic symptoms. Cognitive changes include problems with *memory, attention, concentration, planning, decision making, comprehension,* and *problem solving*. These changes are often gradual at first and are not necessarily related to any specific difficulty, such as a history of problems in math or reading. Although other psychotic symptoms are debilitating, many individuals note cognitive decline as a primary area of concern.

> Imagine if your mind began to get foggy and regular thinking abilities became harder for an unknown reason. And, no matter how much you tried, things only seemed to be getting harder, not easier. Now, couple that with negative symptoms such as low motivation (avolition) and decreased pleasure (anhedonia). Thinking is not only more difficult, but the typical circumstances that would normally help you to persevere on a cognitive task are decreased (e.g., motivation and enjoyment in the task). Now add some very threatening voices and confusing beliefs about being monitored over the course of several months. Envision how this may impact your daily functioning. How would you perform at work or in school? How would this impact your relationships?

ASSOCIATED SYMPTOMS OF A PSYCHOTIC EPISODE

Abnormal Motor Behavior

In some cases, individuals experiencing psychosis may demonstrate *abnormal motor behaviors*. These are unusual patterns of movement that evidence a change in the person's reactivity to his or her environment. Some people may exhibit *physical agitation and restlessness* that may interfere with normal activities. For example, a student may have substantial difficulty sitting still in class despite trying to attend to the material, and he or she might be disruptive to other students and could be asked to leave the room. Conversely, some may experience *catatonia*, a state of reduced reactivity to environmental stimuli. A person experiencing catatonia may appear to be completely unresponsive for extended periods of time, although he or she is clearly conscious. He or she may maintain a rigid posture, either in a conventional position (i.e., sitting or standing) or in a more bizarre posture (i.e., a limb raised, body intertwined, or appearing uncomfortable). When a person is experiencing an episode of catatonia, he or she may be largely unresponsive to others, and may only rarely produce their own verbal or motor responses. In some cases, abnormal motor behavior may appear to be more episodic than other more stable symptoms. For instance, an individual who experiences catatonia may appear less responsive to the environment than most people in general.

However, he or she may also experience several hours or days in which unresponsiveness appears more pronounced.

The restless and agitation described earlier may look similar to hyperactivity seen in attention deficit hyperactivity disorder (ADHD). However, the main difference is an isolation to body movements in psychosis rather than larger movements and actions such as moving around the room. Some abnormal motor movements are side effects of antipsychotic medication. As discussed in Chapter 1, extrapyramidal side effects can present as involuntary tics, jerks, or spasms. These can be easily decreased with adjunctive medications designed to control these involuntary movements.

Poor Insight

Insight refers to an individual's ability to understand the presence of his or her symptoms. It is common that individuals experiencing an episode of psychosis have difficulty identifying and understanding the symptoms of their illness, demonstrating a *lack of insight*. In part, this can be attributed to the nature of psychotic symptoms; that is, they are experienced by the individual as real experiences and are often not recognized as symptoms of an illness at all. Let us take a minute to reflect. How often do you question your own experiences? Most of us assume that the way we perceive the world is accurate. The discomfort experienced by individuals with psychosis is different from the discomfort one might experience from another illness. For instance, consider the discomfort of a stomach virus. Symptoms are experienced as internally located and as a drastic departure from the normal experience. A person is likely to immediately notice stomach distress, nausea, and extreme fatigue, and be able to identify the part of his or her body responsible for the pain. Psychosis (and many other types of mental health symptoms) is different in a number of meaningful ways. First, symptom onset is often relatively gradual and occurs over time, making it difficult for someone to identify a radical change in his or her experience. Individuals who hear voices may initially hear occasional whispers of unintelligible speech, and over the course of months or even years this may progress to more frequent coherent voices making commentary on their life. This gradual evolution often causes symptoms to go unnoticed for some time, and to be experienced as a stable state, rather than as a departure from the norm.

Additionally, the discomfort of psychotic symptoms does not correspond to a physical location in the body, and is not typically interpreted as being internally located. Individuals who experience hallucinations or delusions interpret these sensations as coming from an external source and therefore may not see themselves as having a problem; rather, it is the perceived external stimulus (i.e., the people telling them to hurt themselves or the government agency that is monitoring them) that is problematic. From the perspective of young people with psychosis, *their world has changed, not them.*

An additional complication related to insight is that the symptoms of psychosis are not always experienced as unpleasant. For some individuals, delusional content may be exciting, pleasurable, or amusing. Common examples of this include experiencing a delusion in which they have been given an important mission that will benefit mankind, that they have a special ability to heal others, or that they are destined to become famous for a particular talent. Similarly, if individuals experience hallucinations of voices making amusing comments about those around them, making statements of encouragement, or providing information that they believe is valuable, these will likely be experienced as pleasurable. People who experience psychotic symptoms that are not distressing in nature are unlikely to perceive that something is "wrong" or that their experiences are related to an illness, making the development of insight challenging.

Young adults who experience psychosis vary in their level of insight. Despite the confusing nature of psychotic symptoms, some individuals may be able to retain some insight into the changes that they have experienced. They may occasionally doubt their delusions or the sources of the hallucinations, and may have awareness that these experiences are a departure from normal functioning and the experience of those around them. For instance, a person might note: "These things didn't used to happen to me" or "I know it doesn't make sense, but...." Even within the same person, the level of insight may vary greatly over time. Some individuals may demonstrate a lack of insight during an episode where they are experiencing active symptoms, but on receiving treatment they develop substantial insight. They may be able to discuss their psychosis objectively, look back and identify early warning signs and occasional symptoms that occur as such. Many individuals will fall on some "middle ground" where elements of insight are present, but some domains may be more challenging. Consider the following example:

> Danny recently began to notice a decline in his grades at college, and his motivation to make any changes that would help his academic situation. He was aware that this was somewhat unlike him but was unsure what to make of it. Shortly before finals he began noticing that a persistent tapping noise that he brushed off as tinnitus or a sign of

stress had developed to a louder knocking sound. Danny was checking the door 4 to 5 times a day to find no one standing outside of his door. He also began to wonder if someone was watching him in his dorm room and considered that the knocking was to encourage some action to catch on camera. Danny thought this sounded far-fetched so he confided in his long-term friend and roommate about his experiences. His roommate assured him that no one was knocking and they checked for hidden cameras together and found nothing. However, Danny couldn't shake that feeling that he was being watched at all times, and he was becoming more fearful.

HOW DO SYMPTOMS APPEAR IN DAILY LIFE?

Many of the symptoms associated with a psychotic episode take place in the consciousness of the individual and are not always observable to others. This often results in difficulty identifying if a person is experiencing these particular types of problems. Additionally, due to impairment in insight, individuals may be less likely to alert others to the presence of a problem. Often, people come to mental health care because someone in the young person's life has noted a change in behavior and has expressed concern. In this section, we discuss the manner in which the previously discussed symptoms may be outwardly expressed in the daily life of an adolescent or young adult. But first, some cautionary notes:

- It is important to note that each individual who experiences symptoms has his or her own *unique* experience; however, there are a number of ways in which these symptoms *commonly* manifest in the lives of young people.
- The difficulties that individuals experience during the onset of psychosis can appear similar to other types of problems. It is important not to assume that an individual evidencing the impairments discussed subsequently is experiencing psychosis based on these observations alone. Determination of the presence of psychosis or any other mental health issue requires a diagnostic evaluation to be completed by a qualified professional. However, it may still be beneficial to connect the individual with appropriate resources if distress is present.
- It is important to consider that what might be out of the norm for one person may represent normal behavior for another. The most helpful indicator that an individual may be experiencing psychosis or any

other mental health concern is that there is a notable change in a person's behavior and a decrease in ability to function.

- In addition to a decrease in functioning, some level of distress will also indicate the need for an intervention. Distress can manifest as worry or anxiety, experiences of fear or threat, confusion, and/or signs of harm to self or others either through self-initiated action or risky, impulsive behavior.
- When in doubt, it is "better safe than sorry." If you feel compelled to assist, then we encourage you to do so. A false positive, or an unnecessary referral for assistance, is better than a false negative, or not offering help and support when it is truly needed.

Decline in Academic or Work Performance

For many young people who develop symptoms of psychosis, difficulty functioning in work or at school is the precipitating factor to seeking treatment, whether they are concerned themselves or referred by a concerned other such as a parent, teacher, supervisor, or peer. In addition, the components of a person's life that are most prominent, often school or work, can become a central component of his or her psychotic process. Delusional content is likely to be related to these settings, for instance believing that colleagues or classmates are plotting against him or her. Similarly, hallucinatory content may be particularly concerned with these settings, where voices may make comments about a person's unsatisfactory performance.

Academic Performance

For students experiencing psychotic symptoms, a drop in grades and class attendance is frequently present. This may be gradual in the early stages of a psychotic illness and slowly increase as psychotic symptoms become more prominent. The early changes may appear to reflect a decrease in academic abilities, difficulty with a particular area or subject, or some other cognitive or learning issue. If you remember, we also discussed that negative symptoms typically present before any signs of psychosis and may manifest as low motivation, fatigue, and a general disconnectedness from the education and social demands of the academic environment. As the illness progresses and psychotic symptoms emerge, one can imagine that it would be difficult for young individuals experiencing active symptoms of psychosis to be able to concentrate, organize their thoughts and behavior, and ignore internal stimuli to an extent that would allow them to perform at a high academic level.

Students experiencing symptoms of psychosis may have difficulty attending class and are likely to demonstrate higher than previous (before onset of symptoms) levels of absenteeism. This may be particularly notable for college students, who are likely to have greater autonomy and freedom regarding attendance. The reasons for a drop in attendance may vary. For instance, one person may have significant negative symptoms that make getting out of bed and going to class incredibly difficult and effortful. For others, disorganization may disrupt time management and prioritizing obligations in a way that would allow them to make it to class reliably. Another example may be that a young person experiencing psychosis is concerned about classmates conspiring to embarrass him or her and is too fearful to go to class. When he or she is able to make it to class, the attention and concentration difficulties noted previously are likely to present notable challenges. He or she may have difficulty following lecture material, taking accurate notes, participating in class discussions and remembering to complete assignments, all of which will contribute to a drop in grades.

We have discussed several behavioral changes that may be observable to others. However, some signs may be present in actual academic work, such as odd or disorganized responses to class material or in class discussions. Individuals with active psychotic symptoms may also be observed looking around the room, staring at others, laughing or whispering to themselves, or appearing preoccupied with an unknown presence or stimulus in the classroom.

Work

Similarly, young adults experiencing psychosis who are employed are likely to face a number of challenges. They may lack the organization to reliably get to work on time or to show up for shifts at all. If able to successfully get to work, they may exhibit a number of behaviors that may make them appear forgetful, inattentive, or apathetic. They may be easily sidetracked, start a task and leave it unfinished, or receive directions from a supervisor and not follow through with them. They may appear to "space out" when they should be completing work, or may prioritize tasks in a way that seems strange to others. The same problems with psychotic symptoms that predominate the academic environment apply to the work environment as well. Like academic functioning, negative symptoms or depressed mood may cause a number of difficulties in the workplace. Such symptoms may result in experiencing reduced motivation so that even minor duties feel overwhelming and exhausting. They may have difficulty with timeliness and completing tasks. They are also likely to experience a number of interpersonal difficulties in the workplace. As noted previously, it is often people, places, and situations that are most central in an individual's life that become intertwined in psychotic thought. For people who are employed, they may develop delusional beliefs or hallucinatory content that is in some way related to their job. This could result in behaviors that do not make sense to colleagues and cause problematic interactions with others. For individuals who experience paranoia, the workplace can be a particularly troubling environment. Coworkers and supervisors may note odd behavior and begin to distance themselves from the young person with psychosis. Let us consider an example:

> George works in the mailroom of a large company and hears a voice that he determines belongs to the company's CEO making inflammatory comments about him. He responds by sending the CEO an e-mail demanding that the comments stop so that he can do his job. His behaviors in response to his experiences (which in his mind make perfect sense) appear bizarre, inappropriate, and unprofessional to others.

This distancing, or reaction to the unusual behavior, may only cause the person with psychosis to become even more distrusting of those in the workplace, compounding the situation. On a positive note, some individuals who are employed in positions that lead to relatively low stress and have a notable amount of structure (e.g., stocking shelves) may still be able to complete tasks satisfactorily; however, people in positions with greater responsibility and higher stress (e.g., child-care or supervisory positions) may have difficulty meeting the demands of their position.

Unusual Behavior

Some individuals may develop new interests or habits that may seem "out of the blue" or unusual to others. Often, these new behaviors are related to delusional or hallucinatory content that the person is experiencing. They may seem bizarre or out of place in our understanding of the world, but often, if we could see, hear, or think in line with the individuals' experience, their behaviors might largely make sense to us. They may prioritize these new activities or behaviors over their normal responsibilities such as school or work. They may also develop new habits, such as changes in their sleeping or eating patterns, going to specific places frequently, or becoming very invested in a particular routine. Conversely, they may refuse to do things that they had done without trouble in the past. For instance, a young person experiencing delusional thoughts about his or her movements being monitored via a tracking device attached to the family car may refuse to ride in the car with the rest of the family.

Some people who experience hallucinations may *respond to internal stimuli*. This refers to a person interacting with hallucinatory material of some kind. The appearance of this interaction will vary depending on the mode of the hallucinations. For someone experiencing auditory hallucinations, this could mean that the individual whispers under his or her breath, laughs in a conversation when it is not appropriate, or makes a facial expression that appears to be in response to something not observable to others. In some cases, it may appear that the person is having a full conversation with someone who is not present. Young people experiencing visual hallucinations may follow hallucinatory stimuli with their eyes or respond to them physically (e.g., swatting, reaching out, and moving out of the way). Individuals who experience command hallucinations may begin to discuss concerns or plans related to these demands, or actively avoid people or places if the individuals are concerned about harming themselves or others related to the demand.

Interpersonal Relationships

Young adults with psychosis often have experiences that are frightening and make it difficult to trust or feel connected to other people. This distrust and lack of connection can lead them to respond to others with frustration, skepticism, and anger, or may lead them to avoid people entirely when it is possible. Some individuals may appear to have a lower frustration tolerance; they may appear moody or standoffish. They may be prone to interpersonal conflict or arguments. This is particularly true if the person is challenged on his or her delusional beliefs. For instance, if concerned parents try to comfort their young adult child by ensuring the child that the neighbors are not spying on him or her and are certainly not planning to kill him or her; this well-intended interaction would likely be frustrating to the individual experiencing those thoughts, because for that individual, those experiences are very real.

In addition, young people who experience psychotic symptoms are often overwhelmed by the number of stimuli they experience at a time. Engaging another person introduces an additional stimulus to their already overstimulating environment. They may respond by trying to keep the interaction as brief as possible or by expressing irritation at having to interact. This can often be troubling to those who care about the individuals, as it may seem that they are distancing themselves from people who care about them.

Decline in Caring for Self

Some individuals who experience psychotic symptoms will have difficulty meeting their basic needs in regard to cleanliness, eating, and sleeping. Some individuals may evidence a decline in hygiene and grooming. They may bathe less frequently or only with prompting and may put far less effort into their appearance. They may appear disheveled, with unkempt hair, and wrinkled and dirty clothes. This disorganization in behavior, as previously described, is often mirrored in the person's environment as well. For individuals who live alone, their living situation may become messy or even unsanitary. For young people with psychosis who live with others, cleanliness (or lack of it) is likely to become a point of contention, as the individuals may not be able to keep up with these tasks to the degree that they were previously.

It also is relatively common for young people experiencing psychosis to have fluctuations in their weight and health. Paranoia can contribute to concern about being poisoned; individuals may passively avoid eating, or flatly refuse. Food choices may be restricted to prepackaged foods that are low in nutrition and high in salt, or fatty foods. Disorganization may also contribute to weight changes as the person may not remember when he or she last had a meal and will have difficulty tracking time and food intake. Disorganization often impacts general health as people may forget to take medications and have difficulty keeping up with medical and psychiatric appointments. The latter point is especially true for paranoia as medication and medical treatment can be seen as a conspiracy or harmful to individuals experiencing persecutory delusions or hallucinations.

Disturbance in sleep is also common for young adults with psychosis, particularly if they experience mood disturbances such as depression or mania in addition to psychotic symptoms. Some individuals may sleep far less than they previously did, while others may sleep far more. Some people experience what comes close to a reversal of the sleep–wake cycle, where they are awake all night and sleep all day. Unfortunately, the positive symptoms of psychosis do not follow the typical sleep–wake cycle. Thus, they may be up most of the night due to a steady stream of voices or sounds, or paranoia of threat or harm. Disorganization also disrupts this process as individuals have difficulty keeping a regular routine. Adolescents and young adults with psychosis often need assistance from family and caregivers to maintain healthy routines.

Social Isolation

As noted in the "Interpersonal Relationships" section of this chapter, many individuals with psychosis experience difficulty engaging with other people for a number of reasons. Often, the thoughts and experiences that an individual with psychosis has may make it very difficult to trust and engage with other people. Thus, young people who begin to experience psychotic symptoms often withdraw socially. For example, a person who was previously involved in several clubs at school and had an active social life may begin ignoring calls from friends, canceling plans, and dropping out of activities in which he or she was previously involved. This may occur because of feeling overwhelmed by hallucinations, paralyzed by delusions and being afraid to leave the house, or defeated by negative symptoms.

Often, social isolation is most apparent to those who live with the individual. Parents, roommates, and siblings are often most acutely aware of the changes that occur in an individual's social environment. A high school student who has previously been close to his or her siblings and parents may now come home from school and head straight to his or her room, leaving it only to eat. This individual may slowly distance himself or herself from friends, declining invitations to socialize, instead preferring to be at home on a computer or watching TV.

Increased Substance Use

Some individuals who experience psychotic symptoms may "self-medicate" by using substances. For instance, an individual may increase marijuana use in order to calm himself or herself, and reduce the anxiety and fear caused by paranoia. Or, individuals may find that drinking alcohol helps them to "quiet" the voices for a time and may begin doing it frequently in order to experience relief. Use of prescription drugs may also increase. For instance, a person may begin taking Adderall, Ritalin, or other medications for ADHD in order to combat difficulties with attention and concentration that many people with psychotic symptoms experience. Unfortunately, these medications typically *overstimulate* the individual and can increase psychotic symptoms.

Substance use is a particularly concerning behavior as many substances, both legal and illegal, can worsen or in some cases even bring about symptoms of psychosis. For instance, marijuana, alcohol, and stimulants such as cocaine and Adderall may lead to an increase in symptoms. Similar to the effects on any individual taking these substances, disinhibition and impulsivity increase and rational and logical thoughts decrease in response to drug use in psychotic populations, meaning people may be more likely to engage in risky or socially unacceptable behaviors that they may not otherwise. Unfortunately, new and poorly understood psychotic symptoms in adolescents and young adults complicate the picture, as the effects of substances can increase responses to symptoms such as enacting plans to thwart delusional threats, following through with command hallucinations to harm themselves or others, or deepening depression in response to berating remarks. Many young people with active psychotic symptoms are unable to see the relationship between increased psychosis and drug use, and instead interpret the opposite relationship: Symptoms are increasing, therefore I need to use substance to calm the experience.

Impairment in Concentration and Attention

For young people who are students or working, often one of the first noticeable symptoms is impairment in concentration and attention that impacts their ability to meet task demands. These impairments can occur because of general cognitive decline associated with psychosis or because of the competing presence of other symptoms. Individuals who experience positive symptoms such as auditory hallucinations may have difficulty attending to important things in their environment because they experience competing forces for their attention. They may have difficulty with reading, taking notes, following through with step-by-step instructions, or following lectures or participating in discussions. In conversation, they may not appear to be listening and may need information repeated several times.

Individuals who experience delusions may also have substantial difficulty with attention and concentration. Delusional thought patterns may interfere with the ability to focus. For example, a person who experiences paranoid delusional thoughts about others trying to harm him or her in some way may be preoccupied with these thoughts and unable to concentrate on relevant material. Furthermore, for those who experience

TABLE 2.4

Symptoms of Psychosis in Daily Life: ABI DISC

Academics and work: reduced concentration, difficulty completing tasks
Behavior change: newly developed or absent behaviors compared with previous functioning
Irritability: easy annoyance in response to benign situations or individuals
Decline in self-care: changes in weight, hygiene, and health
Isolation: decreased engagement with friends and family
Substance use: increased use of drugs and alcohol to manage symptoms or "self-medicate"
Concentration and attention: difficulty with focus and completing tasks

paranoia, school or work settings can often be particularly challenging as interacting with large numbers of peers and authority figures may activate delusional thoughts about these people. As you might have gathered, we enjoy mnemonics. The mnemonic ABI DISC outlines the domains of impairment characteristic of a psychotic episode in adolescents and young adults and can be seen in Table 2.4.

SUMMARY

In this chapter and the previous chapter, we have attempted to identify psychosis, in general, and what a psychotic episode may look like across different situations. We have asked you to review a number of symptoms, discussed the different ways the symptoms can manifest across people and situations, and outlined indicators of developing psychotic illness, specifically in adolescents and young adults. We have also detailed the heterogeneity of psychotic illness by describing that there is no real "characteristic" psychotic episode and by introducing the myriad of different ways psychotic illness can present. You may be asking yourself, "How will I ever know if what I'm seeing is psychosis and how will I know when to help?" Luckily, memorizing the various symptoms and presentations is not necessary to help adolescents and young adults with psychosis, or anyone for that matter. Although psychosis is incredibly diverse, *distress* has a common language. There can be any number of reasons why many of the symptoms and behaviors outlined in this chapter can occur.

It is not important for you to know *why* something has occurred or even exactly *what* it is you are seeing when an individual appears in distress or in crisis. We ask only that you act, and apply the "better safe than sorry" approach. Our hope is that more individuals who have not been identified with a psychotic illness will be assisted early in their illness and offered the help they need to achieve recovery as early as possible. If you are reading this book, you are likely to be in a position where you are more likely to encounter an individual in psychiatric distress and have the ability to introduce assistance in some way. Some young people may not need or want help; at worst you have let them know that there are caring people, like you, who are interested in the health and well-being of others and can introduce help in a variety of ways.

For those who are in need of psychiatric assistance to understand and stabilize symptoms and/or to achieve safety, you will have the unique opportunity to introduce them to the idea or possibility that help and recovery are possible by linking them to treatment in some fashion. This process will look different depending on your role, but we can assure you that you can be a critical component in the journey to hope, health, and recovery. In the next chapter, we begin to discuss *how* to approach and engage someone in need of possible assistance or intervention that has been brought to your attention. We introduce different levels of interventions, offer example scenarios, and provide specific strategies for assistance. Throughout the next two chapters, we also hope to empower you to put this information into action by detailing just how important *you* are to this process and by building confidence in your abilities and strengths to make a difference.

REFERENCE

Caplan, J. P., & Stern, T. A. (2008). Mnemonics in a nutshell: 32 aids to psychiatric diagnosis. *Current Psychiatry, 7*(10), 27–33.

CHAPTER **THREE**

How Can You Engage an Individual Identified as Needing Assistance?

Our aim up to this point has been to provide basic and fundamental knowledge that will be helpful in identifying if psychiatric symptoms are present and assisting when there may be concern about psychiatric stability. Intervention may happen in early stages of a psychotic episode where some strange or odd behaviors are present. However, you may find yourself involved in the later stages when there is greater, immediate concern about safety and stability. We expect that the situations we are preparing you for will be confusing, unclear, and perhaps intimidating. We also understand that what we are encouraging you to do may feel awkward or even counterintuitive. Outside of some professions and situations, our culture supports minding our own business and not sticking our noses where they do not belong. We tend to believe that it is neither our place to step in without being asked, nor is it our *problem*. It may actually be perceived as rude, inappropriate, or threatening. So, yes, we are encouraging you to actively ignore many of these social "rules." However, we believe that this approach is acceptable and necessary in certain circumstances, psychiatric crisis being one of them. Moreover, if you are reading this text, you are probably more likely to encounter a psychiatric crisis than the general population and are an important link in the chain toward psychiatric recovery.

Assisting adolescents and adults in a psychiatric crisis encompasses a series of steps: engagement, intervention, and follow-up.

This chapter focuses on developing the first step. In order to effectively intervene and assist, getting the "buy in" from the adolescent or young adult in question can be very important. This may not always happen for a number of reasons, but it is very important to attempt to establish a relationship or some other foundation before moving forward with an intervention. In this chapter, we first discuss what you can expect from individuals who are being approached with concern about their current mental health status. We then guide you through a mini self-assessment to increase awareness about your role, perspective, and approach. Finally, basic communication and engagement skills that are important for this situation are also introduced as a reminder of strategies that are most helpful for delicate and vulnerable situations.

It is expected that every encounter will be different. This is true across different individuals and if you are confronted with the task of helping the same person more than once. Thus, the information in this chapter is best used if reviewed frequently and practiced on a regular basis in some form. We provide examples of different encounters, but believe that you should expect the unexpected. As clinicians who see patients on a regular basis in many different settings, we continue to be surprised by our own patients, and by new patients experiencing symptoms in a unique way. Luckily, there are many "right ways" to engage and assist, and only a few critical "wrong ways." The main objective with any psychiatric crisis is that the individual gets connected to the appropriate help as quickly as possible. For adolescents and young adults in the early stages of illness, this timeline becomes even more critical as duration of untreated illness predicts the level of recovery achieved and the number and severity of future episodes. There will likely be some people you encounter who are not experiencing a psychiatric crisis and for whom psychiatric treatment is not appropriate at this time. However, the goal here is to facilitate connection to a treatment provider who can evaluate the signs and symptoms of distress. Thus, we firmly believe in our approach of "better safe than sorry."

WHAT TO EXPECT WHEN APPROACHING WITH CONCERN

Discussing concerning or problematic behaviors with a young person is never easy. It is common for interactions of this nature to feel threatening and intrusive. Caught in between childhood and adulthood, an adolescent or young adult battles for his or her independence and unique development of self-concept. Individuals in a psychiatric crisis are no different. They too are trying to integrate their experience into a narrative that makes sense while being firmly committed to independence and self-sufficiency. Thus, many of the potential reactions described herewith are very similar to the typical responses of young people when confronted with questions, concerns, and the need for help. However, the bizarre, confusing, and illogical symptoms that can accompany psychiatric crisis complicate these typical responses. Moreover, lack of insight into illness and symptoms further obscures the picture if what you are seeing as problematic or not based on reality is seen by the individual as very real, very rational, and very significant. Remember, it is the world around the individual that appears to have changed and you are part of that world.

The responses discussed in this section are not exhaustive and a number of factors impact the nature of the response. It is not your responsibility to predict, control, or alter the response. Instead, we ask that you enter into these interactions with an open mind, prepared for a myriad of different responses. Moreover, we ask you to be aware of the topic and its potential implications. Even the most psychotic individual is typically aware of "psychosis" and mental health stigma, and most do not want to be identified as such, regardless of the mental health difficulty. As a whole, this chapter discusses important considerations when initiating a delicate conversation with significant implications. In the next chapter, we detail the best strategies for intervention with some modifications for different emotional states and reactions.

TYPICAL RESPONSES

A common response to concern about psychiatric symptoms is *denial* or refusal that what you are discussing is actually occurring. Denial may be present for a number of reasons. If a paranoid belief system is present, denial of any problems at all may "protect" the individual from some perceived threat (i.e., you and the government agency you work for). Paranoia can elicit denial if auditory hallucinations are present that threaten safety if any information is revealed. Denial is also likely to occur if the individual has some insight into his or her symptoms and the illness. After all, what adolescent or adult wants to admit that they hear voices, particularly if they are still trying to make sense of it themselves? See the example that follows:

> Professor Smith observed some very strange behavior in one of the university students he regularly passed on the way to class.

Devan was often seen mumbling to himself and looking down at the ground while walking. Professor Smith noticed that the mumblings had become more intense. Rather than the simple self-dialogue he was known to engage in himself, Professor Smith observed Devan in what appeared to be conversations with another individual. He had also begun to slow his pace when approaching Devan to try to gauge his emotional state. These "conversations" certainly didn't appear pleasant. There was also a notable change in Devan's outward appearance. The once nicely dressed young man now appeared disheveled; he also seemed unaware of the increasingly cool weather. Because he had come to know Devan over the semester due to their regular passing, Professor Smith decided to stop Devan the next time he saw him and inquire about how he was feeling. On a Tuesday morning Professor Smith saw Devan approaching down the sidewalk, like clockwork. He stopped him and said "Good morning." Devan made little eye contact and seemed to be trying to get away from the conversation. Professor Smith then stated, "I've noticed that you appear to be under more distress lately when we pass in the morning. Are you okay?" Devan looked at him wide-eyed and yelled, "I don't know what you're talking about. Mind your own business and leave me alone!"

Defensiveness is another typical response. Subjective experience is personal, important, and real. It is a common reaction to protect our experiences from the judgments of others even if we are judging them ourselves. Discussion or challenge of one's experience can feel very intrusive. Thus, an individual may feel more defensive about the inquiry of the experience more than the experience itself. Consider the following:

Imagine that someone started referring to all of the blue clothing you own as red. "Nice red shirt!" At first, you might be confused and attempt to correct the individual. "What? It's blue." After a while, everyone is referring to your blue clothes as red. You would likely become annoyed, frustrated and more forceful in making your point that your shirt is in fact blue. "Are you kidding? It's blue!" As you become more irritated, the others will become more emphatic in their attempts to convince you that your shirt is indeed red. After all, everyone else agrees, so you must be the one that is wrong. You may choose to continue to stand your ground and continue expressing your difference of opinion, or you may avoid talking about your shirt altogether, knowing deep down that you *know* it is blue.

This example may seem arbitrary and a little silly. However, if you truly try to entertain the notion of this situation, you might find yourself identifying with how irritated you might become when someone tries to convince you that something you believe to be true (or know from your experience) is not. If such a minor thing could cause us to become irritated, imagine what it might be like if the subject were something that was truly core to your life experience: someone telling you that you are not who you think you are, that you are not employed in the job that you believe you are, or that there is no music playing even though you hear it. To each of us, our experience of the world is real and meaningful. This is true of individuals with psychosis as well. What is believed, thought, felt, heard, and seen are deeply real, even if they may not be to others. It is important to respect the reality of a person's experience as much as possible, and to anticipate defensiveness when it is threatened.

Fear and *anxiety* may present themselves in a variety of ways when a young person with psychosis is confronted with the overtness of his or her symptoms. Fear and anxiety about others' reactions to the symptoms and their response are likely to occur. For example, an individual may be concerned about being "locked in a hospital" or being punished. Moreover, an individual may be concerned how the symptoms themselves may change or manifest. For example, command hallucinations may have threatened harm if there were any divulgence of the private conversations. Will they be angry? What will happen if they are? Individuals who believe that they are working for a private conglomerate to protect against some conspiracy may feel that they have breached privacy and will then be punished.

Closely tied to fear or anxiety, an individual being confronted with concern may display *anger* or *aggression*. Unfortunately, this has become the response that most readily comes to mind when people think about psychosis. However, this is not necessarily the most common response of individuals experiencing psychosis, and when anger or aggression are present, it is most often in response to perceived threat. Consider for a moment a situation similar to the red shirt scenario; that is, if someone came up to you right now and told you that what you perceive (e.g., the words on this page, the view from the nearest window, the sounds from your environment) was not real. Wait, what? Of course, that is not the case, but why doesn't that person believe you, and why are they so insistent? Questioning one's own perceptions and reality is very frightening. In addition to the vivid sensory experiences that comprise hallucinations, the content of hallucinations is also very real, as we have described previously. Therefore, if an individual is being informed via auditory hallucinations that someone is out to harm him or her, or if an individual possesses an elaborate delusional system that a conspiracy against his or her life is underway, a private conversation with a concerned parent, teacher, or counselor about odd behaviors and beliefs will likely be received with fear or anger, and some verbal or physical aggression may follow. In the "Dos and Don'ts" section of Chapter 4 we offer suggestions to facilitate the most productive interaction possible, even in the presence of many unknowns and unpredictable responses including anger.

Due to symptom severity, limited insight, and/or emotional distress, *confusion* about the concern being presented and the symptoms being discussed may occur. Positive symptoms, negative symptoms, and disorganization can all contribute to confusion about what is "real" and what is part of the illness. Thus, individuals may be confused about behaviors or thoughts that appear odd to others but very real and logical to them. Consider the following example:

> Celia's soccer coach, Coach Taylor, had recently become
> concerned about her star forward's notable behavior
> changes. At first the changes were small—distraction at
> practice and during team meetings where Celia seemed
> to be off in her own world. Lately, she had also become
> more withdrawn. The once bubbly sophomore now sat by
> herself and rarely chatted with her teammates. She started
> wearing long sleeves and pants under her practice uniform
> for "protection" and recently requested to be replaced
> in her typical starting position by another player due to
> feeling "uncomfortable." The odd look on her face kept
> Coach Taylor from pushing any further. Over the last week,
> Celia stopped coming to practice and her mother called
> to report that she was "under the weather and unable to
> play or practice." Coach Taylor asked to meet with Celia
> after school one afternoon. She shared her concerns about
> Celia's altered approach toward the game she loved and
> what seemed like genuine fear on the field. Celia responded
> with a blank look, stating "I just feel uncomfortable...and
> weird. But nothing is wrong. I'm sure everyone feels like
> that sometimes."

Negative symptoms and disorganization can also impair reality-based thinking through difficulty engaging with the environment (e.g., negative symptoms) and organizing and communicating thoughts, feelings, and behaviors (e.g., disorganization). Imagine the following example of negative symptoms and disorganization.

Kim's tutor finally decided to approach her about observing Kim talking to herself on multiple occasions when working alone on assignments. The tutor brought up the subject during their next scheduled meeting. She told Kim what she had seen and asked her if everything was okay. Kim had been increasingly withdrawn and quiet over the last several months but the tutor chalked it up to teenage "angst" and assumed there were friend or relationship troubles. However, Kim's response to the tutor's concern was strange. She just looked back blankly. Kim did share that she was having some strange experiences—a voice had started commenting on her behaviors. However, Kim's expression and tone of voice were without emotion; this was not something the tutor would expect from someone who just acknowledged hearing voices! In fact, Kim barely reacted. It was at this point that the tutor noticed just how much Kim's demeanor had changed. There wasn't much of anything that brought out a strong emotion or reaction, and her motivation to complete schoolwork had certainly dwindled. The tutor was unsure just how much Kim was affected by internal experiences.

This section aims to illustrate a number of different responses that may be helpful to prepare for when approaching an adolescent or young adult with concern. It will be hard to predict exactly how individuals will respond, even if you know them well. Moreover, the picture is likely to be more complex in that there will be more than one type of response, and the reaction may shift throughout the conversation. Regardless, we hope this provides a foundation for preparing to initiate this delicate conversation and for being somewhat flexible to best accommodate the emotional response.

IMPORTANT CONSIDERATIONS PRIOR TO INTERVENTION

The reaction to concern about psychiatric crises, safety, and potential intervention may be quite varied. There are a number of different factors that contribute to this including the context and the environment, the severity and type of symptoms present, and the relationship between the young person and the responder.

Context

When attempting to initiate a conversation regarding concerns about one's mental health, it is important to consider when and how an individual is being approached. Are they in a place where they feel safe such as their home, doctor's office, or a "neutral" site? Is the encounter occurring during a planned meeting or is the encounter somewhat unexpected? The impact of context is not likely to differ from any other situation where a person is being approached about concern for them. In general, we accept concern and intervention better when the environment is safe and predictable, and where collaboration appears present or possible. It is likely to be difficult to plan or control the environment in many circumstances, and the situation may not be conducive to an organized approach. However, it is important to consider and acknowledge the impact that environment may have on an individual's response to a potential interaction or intervention.

State of the Illness

The severity and type of symptoms will also affect the initial stages of intervention. Deciding to intervene is likely in response to some concerning symptom or behavior that may or may not be present at the time when a planned interaction is initiated. It is important to be aware that an individual's symptoms will impact responsiveness to some degree in the same way a subjective, internal experience impacts any of our responses to different situations. Moreover, insight into the illness and its effects will also impact an individual's understanding of the symptoms concerning you and their motivation to participate in any form of treatment for said symptoms. Symptoms such as paranoia may elicit greater defensiveness, feelings of threat, and grandiosity. Depending on the nature of the paranoid belief system, individuals may have widely varied responses to intervention or treatment.

Relationships

In addition to the context (e.g., environment, type and severity of symptoms) the relationship with the responder (e.g., you!) is important and there are three considerations that we believe are significant: (a) Is the responder known to the adolescent or young adult? (a) Did the responder witness the concerning account firsthand or is the encounter based on secondhand information? and (c) Does the responder represent an authority figure compared with someone in a neutral position? Each of these situations is addressed individually.

KNOWN VERSUS UNKNOWN RESPONDER

The nature of the responder's relationship with the individual of concern is quite significant. The concerns of a trusted individual are likely to carry more weight than concerns from an unknown party. This may not always be evident initially as there will be a number of different responses that are likely to occur in response to the kinds of discussions we are preparing you for in this text. However, *familiarity* often equates to *predictability*. Even if the person is caught off guard, confused, or defensive in response to your concerns, the stable and known features of you and the previous interactions will likely provide a buffer even if this is hard to see or experience. Consider your own experience receiving upsetting news or hearing about a strange and confusing state of events that impacts you directly. You will likely be looking (and may be clinging) to people, environments, and routines that are familiar, and thus calming. The same notion applies here.

Conversely, if you are in the tough position to approach someone who is mostly or completely unknown to you there will be some challenges and the responses described earlier may be more prominent or intense. The individuals being approached are likely to be receiving confusing or, in their eyes, illogical news by someone who (seemingly) knows nothing about them or their situation. There is very little you can do to *change* this scenario. In some cases, it may be helpful to acknowledge this shortcoming in the interaction (e.g., "I know we don't know each other very well, so this might sound a little strange coming from me..."). In addition, there are important communication skills that will improve this situation. These verbal and nonverbal skills are discussed in the next section of this chapter.

PRIMARY VERSUS SECONDARY OBSERVER

The second relationship factor that we would like you to consider is the responder's perspective of the identified problem. There are certainly benefits of observing the concerning behavior or symptoms yourself prior to initiating a conversation about concern. At the very least, this will allow the responder to provide a context for the concern ("Do you remember yesterday in class when…") and some details about the behavior or occurrence that will help establish some foundation for the conversation. It is still expected that some emotional response will occur even with these elements present, but this may help establish a reality-based, foundational conversation.

There may be times when your organization's policy, or your personal comfort level, requires that you report any concerns to another individual designated to respond to crises, high-risk situations, and delicate circumstances. This approach may be beneficial in that the designated individual may have some experience or expertise with these types of situations. However, adding a new person into the mix can increase suspicion and paranoia in the adolescent or young adult. Additionally, feelings of threat and fear may emerge. Consider the following example:

> Skylar had been experiencing intensifying paranoia about an unknown threat that was disrupting his ability to concentrate in his freshman literature course. When reading the assigned text the words on the page often jumbled together, and at times presented a very macabre story about death and persecution. The story Skylar was reading appeared very different than the story being reviewed in class and the discussion questions presented for homework were completely unrelated to the story. Skylar began to wonder why he was assigned such a bizarre and disturbing assignment while other students were assigned a different piece. As his fear and feelings of threat increased he decided to write a letter to the professor about his disgust toward the text and his anger about being singled out and "targeted" for an unknown reason. A couple of weeks later, the department chair contacted Skylar for a meeting. At the meeting the department chair asked Skylar if they could discuss the letter he turned in to his professor. Skylar immediately felt unsafe, and his concern that his professor was plotting to get him removed from her course was becoming more and more evident.

AUTHORITY VERSUS NONAUTHORITY FIGURE

The final consideration that we believe is important is the significant difference between being approached by an authority versus a nonauthority figure. This can be a tricky distinction as most adults can be viewed as "authority" figures or having some control, power, or "say so" over the adolescent or young adult. Again, there may not be anything that can be done about who intervenes given a particular organizational policy or crisis plan. However, it is important to acknowledge that the role of the responder will likely have some impact on the adolescent or young adult and how he or she perceives and reacts to the discussion. In the preceding example, the department chair approached Skylar. It would be expected that the department chair has some additional influence on Skylar's academic record and future. Skylar may have had a different response if he were approached by the professor or by the guidance counselor.

BASIC ENGAGEMENT BEHAVIOR

We hope we have given you an idea of some important considerations and expectations after you have made the decision to approach someone about concern for psychotic symptoms. The decision to intervene on any level carries implications, both positive and negative, for everyone involved and particularly the individual being approached. Given the nature of the situation, it is difficult to develop a detailed plan about exactly what will happen. Resistance will very likely happen at some level, and there are many unknowns to be prepared for and many variables to consider. However, there are certainly some basic factors that, if implemented, will certainly set the stage for a more successful interaction, which will hopefully facilitate connection to some form of treatment.

Although there may be several issues in this interaction that are outside of your control, your approach and response are things you can control. If nothing else you can create an environment that feels safe. Keep in mind that this interaction that you have decided to facilitate may go nowhere—perhaps, despite your best efforts, no discussion of symptoms or distress occurred and no engagement with care was made. However, you still have a very critical role as you may be the initial interaction that helps support a future interaction that *does* eventually facilitate engagement with care. At the very least, you are helping to set the stage.

Thus far in this chapter we have discussed situations and variables that are critical to consider before an adolescent or individual is approached. The last section of this chapter is focused on verbal and nonverbal skills that will assist in engaging the adolescent or young adult in a conversation that is *more likely* to support collaboration on a plan for seeking treatment. You will notice that these appear to be very basic skills that are helpful in virtually any interaction with anyone of any age group. They are! In fact, they are so basic that we do not always pay attention to ensure that we are utilizing them in everyday conversation. Although we can usually get away with this in familiar conversation, using these skills in an unfamiliar or delicate conversation can be very useful. These basic engagement skills will be discussed in two parts—verbal and nonverbal skills.

Verbal Behavior

Verbal skills are exactly as they sound: They have to do with *what* we say and *how* we say it. We would like to focus on style of questioning, tone and prosody, and empathy. The goal of these factors is to create an environment that feels as calm and open as possible.

SIMPLE AND DIRECT QUESTIONS

When first approaching an individual identified as demonstrating concerning thoughts or behaviors, you will likely be anxious, scared, or confused. Regardless, you will have a lot on your mind and many questions that you will want to address. We suggest preparing two to three questions to start. This is encouraged for a few different reasons. First, it is important to stay focused: What is it that you *most* need to know in order to successfully negotiate an engagement plan to connect with a provider? Second, identifying two to three questions decreases the likelihood that you and the adolescent or young adult will feel overwhelmed by the interaction itself. Firing questions at anyone, under any circumstance, heightens the intensity and the emotion of the interaction. That is certainly not necessary here. Finally, focusing on only a few questions helps provide structure and expectations for what could be a complicated interaction. Examples of simple and direct questions are found throughout Chapter 4.

Hopefully, you will be able to engage the individual in a conversation that allows for a detailed discussion of recent symptoms and experiences. However, it is more likely that the adolescent or young adult will quickly become tight-lipped for a myriad of different reasons (e.g., anxiety, paranoia, fear of being hospitalized, fear of not being believed). Identifying two to three questions would allow you to get the most important information before either party is overwhelmed. Moreover, it may allow for some bargaining, such as saying something to the effect of, "I know you don't feel like talking to me about this. How about if I limit this conversation to two questions and then I'll give you space?" As always, you may get resistance, but this certainly sounds more manageable to an adolescent or young adult than a free-for-all!

You may not have time to "prepare" two to three questions for every scenario. In fact, you may have no time to prepare if the psychotic episode is more acute and a crisis. Thus, we encourage you to consider your current position and responsibilities and identify two to three standard questions that you may need to know to facilitate engagement with care. These may be different for a campus policeman versus a high school guidance counselor versus a residence hall adviser.

In addition to preparing a set of focused questions we also want you to consider how you present the questions. In order to be most effective we recommend very simple and direct questions: sentences with a clear question and as few words as possible to reflect the inquiry. We advise against distractors such as large words or wordy explanations or caveats. Phrasing as open-ended questions are also more likely to be helpful as they will illicit more information than questions asking for "yes" or "no" responses.

TONE AND PROSODY

After considering *what* you want and/or need to know, it is important to think about how to best get that information. We want to highlight *how* the questions and any other information are delivered. Tone refers to quality of voice and prosody refers to the rhythm and intonation of speech. These two factors are important because they will help set the "vibe" of the interaction. An individual who is experiencing psychotic symptoms is likely experiencing a number of different emotions. You can greatly assist in the interaction by modeling stability and calmness through your speech. This is achieved by using a neutral tone that is not overly laden with emotion, thus, not too "high" (e.g., happy, excited, anxious) or too "low" (e.g., scared, sad, angry).

Prosody is also another tool that can be used to demonstrate calmness and stability. This is achieved through a moderate pace where you are not speaking too quickly or too slowly. The speed of our speech can induce emotion very easily. For example, speaking very quickly may suggest anxiety or worry, while speaking too slowly can induce confusion and distress.

Take a moment to practice. Out loud to yourself ask, "Are you going to the store?" Think about how you said that sentence, naturally, without any further instruction. Now, ask the same question very quickly. Next, ask the same question in a higher volume or tone. Lastly, put these two together and ask the question at a quick pace and in a high volume. Reflect on how those different scenarios may suggest different meanings.

EMPATHY

Empathy refers to the notion of being able to put yourself in someone else's shoes to try and understand his or her experience. This is different from sympathy, which reflects understanding what someone is going through because you have been through it yourself. Empathy is critical to the practice of psychology and psychological intervention, but it is also very helpful to use in everyday life and conversation. The goal of empathy is to *demonstrate* your investment in trying to understand the other person's situation or experience even though this cannot be achieved completely, and this can be done in a number of different ways.

First and foremost, show that you are listening by responding to the adolescent's or young adult's statements with a brief display of understanding such as "Yes," "Okay," or "I see." These brief statements demonstrate that you are listening to what is being said. A complementary strategy to also use is to reflect that you are not only listening, but that you also *hear* what is being said. This is achieved by repeating verbatim or giving a summary of what the adolescent or young adult has said. For example, if after approaching an adolescent or young adult and sharing your concern about paranoia, the individual describes that he or she has recently been receiving messages through news reports that appear to be addressed to him or her, you may say something like, "Okay. You have been watching the news and it feels like someone is trying to send you a message through the news reports." A final way to demonstrate empathy is to summarize all that you have heard and check for accuracy. For example, if we use the previous example, you might check for accuracy by saying, "Do I have that right?" and "Did I miss anything?"

This is certainly not an exhaustive list of empathic strategies. Ultimately the goal is to show that you have dedicated your undivided attention and that you are interested in what the person has to say. Remember, you may get responses that are more resistant or less organized. No matter how the adolescent or young adult is responding, the empathic strategies we have just described can and should be implemented. What you are reflecting in the *hearing* stage may not make logical sense if you are summarizing an illogical thought or belief. However, the goal of this stage of the exchange is to build trust and collaboration, and demonstrate understanding of *their* experience.

Nonverbal Behaviors

In addition to verbal features of the conversation, there are also nonverbal variables that can impact how information, questions, and the general understanding of the interaction are perceived. We can convey a great deal without ever saying a word. Surely you can reflect on some of your own experiences when a facial experience or stance spoke volumes without a word being uttered! We describe the potential effects of these and other nonverbal behaviors as follows.

BODY LANGUAGE

The way we present ourselves in different situations communicates a significant amount of information about how we perceive the environment, how we feel about being a part of it, and, perhaps, how we feel toward other individuals who may be involved or present. We would like to draw attention to some very simple but important gestures to notice when approaching a young person with psychosis about a delicate topic. The first is an open versus closed stance. Crossing our arms and legs and generally minimizing our physical presence may convey disinterest, fear, or a general sense of not wanting to be involved. Although you may actually feel this way about the encounter, exhibiting this to the individual you are trying to assist will likely decrease the other's interest and engagement, and may cause other negative feelings such as confusion, worry, or fear. Conversely, approaching with arms at your sides and taking up more "space" demonstrates interest and commitment in being present at that moment.

Although the type of interaction we have been discussing will likely be somewhat challenging and confusing for everyone, it is important to *appear* as calm as possible. Remember, you will be modeling the feeling, so to speak. Thus, try to keep nervous habits to a minimum such as shaking legs, wringing hands, or nail biting. Again, those are perfectly natural responses to an uncomfortable and anxiety-provoking situation, but they may not be helpful toward the goal at hand.

EYE CONTACT

Good eye contact also demonstrates your interest and investment in the interaction. In addition to the reflective and summary statements we described in the previous section, maintaining eye contact shows that you are listening. We have a tendency to look down or look away when confronted with information that makes us uncomfortable or upset, and this is not a message we recommend conveying to an adolescent or young adult who may be looking for support and/or who is already experiencing these feelings himself or herself. While we might expect poor eye contact from a young person in psychiatric crisis, this is about demonstrating an attentive and understanding stance, regardless of the abilities of the young person at the time.

PERSONAL SPACE

Although the skills and behaviors we have briefly discussed here do not represent an exhaustive list, we feel that they are the most critical and perhaps the easiest to "control" when preparing for or engaging in this interaction. The last behavior we would like to discuss is personal space. This is something that is usually a personal preference for each of us. This is true for everyday situations, and even more so during periods of crisis or overwhelming events. Moreover, these boundaries may actually shift in more intense situations. Thus, it is important to be aware that during periods of crisis, emotional and physical space will be important. Therefore, keep this in mind when approaching the adolescent or young adult. The concerns being shared and the notion of pursuing treatment may already be overwhelming and space will likely be needed to process the information.

Another consideration when providing personal space is your safety. As we have discussed previously, it is hard to predict the reaction of the adolescent or young adult with psychosis; he or she may respond in any number of ways and for any number of reasons. One potential response is anger or aggression and these reactions may be conveyed in words or actions. A person may respond to anger, fear, or confusion by pacing, moving or throwing items, or violence. Although physical aggression is unlikely, it is always possible. Thus, it is also important for you to provide space for yourself. If it is necessary to move close to or make physical contact with the young adult, it may be helpful to ask permission ("Do you mind if I sit next to you?" "I can see your arm is hurt, is it okay if I use the first-aid kit to bandage it?") in order to allow the young adult to feel a sense of control over what is happening in the situation.

SUMMARY

The goal of this chapter was to provide initial considerations when preparing to assist an adolescent or young adult. These topics are important to consider before you even approach this person, and in the first few moments of the interaction to facilitate a conversation and build a foundation toward collaboration on a treatment-seeking plan. Exhibits 3.1 to 3.4 provide some fictional examples of scenarios that may be of help. I am sure you have noticed that there are many uncertainties and "what ifs," and there are likely scenarios that you have imagined or actually encountered that were not exactly captured here. However, we believe that the topics covered in this section represent information that can be generalized across situations and represent the most common occurrences. Moreover, we strongly feel that if you consider the areas that we have discussed in this chapter you will have the best chance of facilitating a successful interaction, even in the presence of unexpected and unfamiliar situations.

EXHIBIT 3.1: **CHRISTOPHER**

Christopher is a 19-year-old male who graduated high school 2 months ago. He recently began working at a local dry cleaner at the encouragement of his mother to "stay busy" after school. Although Christopher was excited about having some extra money in his pocket, he was becoming increasingly uncomfortable at work and this was starting to affect his performance.

Christopher was always known as a happy child with a number of different interests and hobbies. However, he preferred solitary activities and never really had many friends. Because he seemed content to play, his parents did not experience much concern about their son. Christopher was a good student with average grades and particularly enjoyed history and literature. Reading about these topics was one of his favorite activities. Overall, Christopher had a relatively normal childhood with no major areas of concern.

Christopher's parents got divorced when he was 16 years of age and his father moved several states away. Although they were still in touch regularly, this change had a notable effect on Christopher. He began to withdraw to his room and spend a lot of time with the door closed. He did not want to attend school and his grades were slowly declining. Christopher's mother chalked it all up to some mild depression and normal teenage angst. Nothing seemed out of the ordinary to her given his age and the recent changes. However, Christopher's grades continued to suffer and he barely graduated with his classmates. Christopher's mother assumed that he must be doing some schoolwork while he was locked in his room, but she learned shortly before his 12th-grade year that it was not the case. It took a significant amount of time and effort to achieve barely passing grades during his final year. Christopher's mother also noticed Christopher whispering to himself when he was walking through the house or riding with her in the car. She could also hear him talking while he was in his room. Again, she concluded that this was likely a normal response to stress and thus did not ask questions or pursue these specific behaviors further. Whenever she generally inquired about her son's well-being, he stated, "I'm fine, just stressed."

Meanwhile, Christopher had begun to hear comments about his difficulties in school. At first he assumed it was his own thoughts and "thinking" about his trouble in trigonometry and his need to try harder. However, the thoughts became louder and more frequent, and he began to make out a distinct voice that did not sound like his own. He also had trouble sleeping because the thoughts never seemed to shut off. Christopher kept himself distracted by wearing headphones and turning the music up to drown out the voice. He never told his mother or father about these experiences because he did not want them to worry or to get in his business. Christopher was able to graduate but it took considerably more effort than he had to put in before. Because of increasing academic difficulty over the last few years, Christopher decided to take a break from school and work before applying to college. He took the job at the dry cleaner to make some money while he prepared for his next steps. He was hopeful that now that school was finished the voice would stop.

Initially, Christopher was feeling good while working. He was still very tired during the day and felt as if his mind was always "turned on" while he slept, but the voice had quieted. However, a month or so into his new job the voice returned. It was subtle at first but then was loud and commenting on his behavior at the dry cleaner. At first, they were just comments such as "You are putting the clothes on hangers," or "You are checking out a customer." The voice then escalated to making nasty comments such as "You are no good at this job, someone should fire you," and "Look at Justine; she is working so much faster than you." At first, Christopher tried to ignore the voice by blocking it out with headphones. The comments also motivated him to work harder. However, over time, these negative comments took a toll on Christopher and he started to have negative thoughts about himself and his abilities. He started to believe the voice and began to notice all the ways in which Justine and other employees were excelling. He also noticed that his supervisor always seemed to be watching him specifically. He just knew that at any point he was going to get reprimanded or even fired. Instead of feeling motivated as he was initially, Christopher started to not want to go to work. He began to experience anxiety about going in and thus would show up late or not show up at all. One day after checking out a customer, the voice stated, "Maybe you should kill yourself, and then you wouldn't be a problem." Christopher was very shocked by this at first; he never had a thought like that before. However, the voice just kept saying things like this over and over, no matter what Christopher did to show disagreement or block it out.

In the meantime, Christopher's mother began to notice her son's change in mood and demeanor. He did not want to go to work and just wanted to lie in bed all day. When she would inquire or show concern Christopher would say things like, "There's no point; I'm not good at that job. I'm not good at anything, really." As the weeks went on, he eventually started talking about killing himself because he was "no good" and "will never go anywhere." He even started blaming himself for his father leaving. She became very concerned about her son's well-being and safety. One day, she received a call from Christopher's supervisor after he had not shown up for work 4 days in a row. He expressed concern about Christopher and shared that he had observed Christopher talking to himself at work and "arguing" with someone who was not there. Christopher's mother had not shared with anyone that she too noticed this behavior increasing. Not only was it scary, she remembered a similar experience with her aunt when she was a little girl and it scared her.

Christopher's mother decided to talk to her son about her concerns. She stated that she noticed that he seemed to be feeling down and was having very negative and scary thoughts. Although she was nervous, she also told him that she noticed that he was talking to himself. Christopher seemed surprised at her observations. After several minutes of silence he shared that a man living in the vacant storefront next to the dry cleaner was talking to him at work. He had even found a way to talk to Christopher even when he was not at work through some means, although Christopher was not sure how. Christopher stated that the man was showing him what a burden he was on others and was helping him think of a plan to take his life. Christopher stated that he did not tell anyone because he knew they would try to stop him. However, Christopher shared that he was not sure he wanted to take his life. After all, he was feeling better, and happy, a few years ago. Hoping that her son wanted to get help, Christopher's mother tried to get her son to agree to see his physician, but Christopher refused and stated that the man was probably following him from the storefront and the man may hurt anyone who tries to help. She then asked her son if he was really thinking about hurting himself and he stated, "That's really my only option at this point." She started to express more concern when Christopher raised his voice and stated, "Mom, there is nothing you can do and it's really not your business. Get out!" Christopher's mother left her son in his room feeling very scared. He seemed pretty set on his decision and she was afraid to force the conversation. From her days as an EMT (emergency medical technician) she remembered that her state had a crisis line. She decided to call to get some insight into what she should do next.

Discussion. In this example, it is clear that Christopher is hearing voices, and has been hearing them for some time. At first they were subtler and less bothersome, but they escalated to the point where he was being commanded to harm himself. This is a typical course for these symptoms; they may be infrequent and quiet at first, but then become more persistent and distressing. The stress and impact of the auditory hallucinations caused a marked change in Christopher's behaviors as he tried to cope (e.g., withdrawing and avoiding). He also began to have some associated delusional beliefs about how this was happening. Christopher's mother had noticed a change but did not say anything for a few reasons. At first, the odd behaviors seemed normal and typical odd behavior for a teenage boy. Later she did not say anything because she did not want to believe that what happened to her aunt may also be happening to her son. Denial is not uncommon in family members and caregivers as well. Luckily, the supervisor decided to reach out and share his concern about his employee. This helped initiate an open discussion about what was happening to Christopher. Christopher's mother approached her son calmly and shared what she noticed about him. Having a conversation like this in a safe and calm environment is very helpful, if it is an option. Moreover, sharing what has been observed in an open, empathic way allows a discussion to develop more easily. When Christopher demonstrated some anger and shared that he was thinking of taking his life, his mother did not challenge or agitate him further with questions. When he refused help she had a feeling that it was not just the physician's help, it was *anyone's* help. Thus, to protect her son she called the local crisis line for assistance. Her hope was that some of the tougher questions could be asked in an environment where her son would be safe and where professionals could determine what was going on and what help he may need.

EXHIBIT 3.2: **JENELLE**

Jenelle recently began her junior year of high school. She was known to be an excellent student who was always involved in a number of activities. Tennis was Jenelle's favorite way to relieve stress when school and other extracurricular activities became overwhelming. She joined her high school tennis team as a freshman and her tennis team was like a little family. Jenelle was able to open up to her coaches and teammates about stress at school and at home, and they were quick to point out when her stress level appeared to affect her tennis game. It was a great relationship.

Despite the closeness that had developed within the team over the last 2 years, Jenelle was withholding something important from her team. Although they knew her well, she did not think they would "get it" because she did not quite understand it herself. Jenelle was generally prone to stress given the number of activities she was involved in. However, she began to feel more pressure lately and she could not quite put her finger on the cause. It started subtly enough—she was feeling compelled to avoid certain driving routes to school and felt like something "bad" may happen if she did not comply. Jenelle chalked this up to "intuition." However, she was feeling more and more "controlled" over time and the "bad" feeling had gradually morphed into a feeling that the world would somehow be in trouble if she did not travel a particular route to school and home. This was greatly affecting her ability to get to school on time and get to tennis practice.

Jenelle did not share these experiences with anyone, fearing that divulging them would in turn cause harm to others. Unfortunately, she was feeling more and more trapped as other behaviors and decisions began to feel "wrong" also. How Jenelle ate her meals, how she completed her assignments, and whom she spoke to were all feeling delegated by an unknown person or group of people. After watching a news program about a recent government hacking scheme Jenelle began to feel personally targeted and became convinced that she was being sought, specifically, for unknown reasons and that a disaster may ensue if she did not continue within the "restrictions" she had been experiencing.

Jenelle's coach, Coach Black, noticed that Jenelle was arriving late for practice on a pretty regular basis. At first, she accepted "feeling overwhelmed" as an excuse for tardiness. However, Coach Black had seen Jenelle stressed before and this seemed different. Tennis used to be a stress reliever for Jenelle and now she could barely focus at practice. She was distracted in between plays. The most significant thing that Coach Black noticed was that tennis itself seemed stressful and, what was worse, no longer enjoyable.

Jenelle managed to maintain some control over this experience for several months and not letting it affect her daily life too much. However, the feelings of "responsibility" for the lives of others was becoming too much to bear. Jenelle was feeling pressured carrying out even the most benign tasks, feeling that the "wrong" decision would mean death for mankind. When she began to feel like she could not go to tennis without risking the lives of millions, she began to feel hopeless. She called Coach Black to quit the team, feeling no choice but to make this sacrifice. Coach Black asked for a meeting in person to discuss such a big decision. Jenelle reluctantly agreed; it was the least she could do. On the morning of the meeting, Jenelle was predictably late due to driving well out of her way to get to school in response to controlling thoughts. Coach Black shared her concerns with Janelle and asked if they could go to the guidance counselor's office. Janelle thanked Coach Black for her concern but stated that she could handle things on her own. After all, what could the guidance counselor understand about being responsible for humanity's survival?

Discussion. Jenelle's experience outlines a relatively common course in the development of delusions and paranoia. A delusional system can start subtly with uneasy feelings, as was the case with Jenelle. Over time, they can gain momentum as the symptoms increase and other situations and experiences are included and perceived as "support" for the delusional thought process. Similar to the case with Jenelle, the events and "evidence" that intensify paranoia and strengthen a delusion are often illogical. The absence of logic or reason may be seen in the relationship across events (e.g., government hacking scheme and risk of mortality for millions of people) and in the power that an individual or force may have in preventing or controlling a situation (e.g., Jenelle's responsibility to save everyone by doing a number of benign tasks). Although it may seem obvious to most that these ideas simply cannot be, when in the midst of a delusional belief system nothing can be further from the truth.

Jenelle's tennis coach began to notice changes early on but assumed that they were related to some other cause. It is not uncommon to assume several other causes of odd or bizarre thoughts and behaviors before mental illness. When mental illness is considered, psychosis is not usually the first guess. When Coach Black did become concerned, she attempted to connect Jenelle with the school guidance counselor. Although Jenelle refused, Coach Black has an established relationship with Jenelle and therefore may be able to continue this conversation in the future as well as monitor any additional changes. Coach Black may also decide to report her concerns to the school counselors anyway so they can be aware of any behavioral issues or concerning changes. Coach Black is not bound by confidentiality and Jenelle did not disclose anything personal that may make Coach Black question whether or not she could share. If Coach Black continues to be concerned, that should be her next step.

EXHIBIT 3.3: **SANDRA**

Sandra had recently begun to feel very uncomfortable when home alone at her apartment. She had loved having her own space and relished the idea that she could come home after work to a place all her own. However, she began feeling very strange when stepping into her apartment, almost as if an ominous cloud had washed over her. At first, she just brushed it off as an odd occurrence and that worked for a few months. She would turn up the sound on the television or radio to distract herself from feeling so uncomfortable. However, the persistence of the feeling led her to begin to worry that something was going on. Maybe she was being watched? Initially, that notion comforted her as she was finally able to explain the strange feeling. However, it was not long before feeling "watched" began to feel scary. Who was watching her, and why? She began peering out her windows and stepping out of her front door to see who may be standing there or walking by. Sandra started to notice that every time she looked out her door or window *someone* was there! What is even worse, it was not even the same person every time! Sandra went from being comfortable at home to being afraid to leave!

Sandra's "peering" out the window slowly turned methodical; the goal was to make as little movement as possible so as not to be detected. She began taking notes of what she saw and when, hoping to find a pattern ("Yesterday a blue car was parked in the front space, but today it is red..."). Everything seemed to have meaning! In the meantime, Sandra had started going into work when it was still dark and not coming home until it was dark again—anything to not be spotted. Sandra still had not figured out why she was being watched but certainly could not take any chances. After a while, she started calling out from work more frequently, afraid that she may miss something important at home or that her strategy for avoiding those watching her would be discovered.

Sandra's concern started to intensify as the situation progressed over the course of several months. She kept the lights off most of the time and used a flashlight at night. She minimized any need to leave the house. Sandra also began neglecting people in her life. She was concerned about using her phone in case it may be tapped. Sandra had been texting with family and friends but slowly began using her phone less and less, to the point where she eventually kept it off completely. It was not worth the risk. Whoever was watching her may also find a way to get to the people whom she loved.

After 2 months of missed rent, Sandra's landlord became concerned. It certainly was not like Sandra to miss rent and now her phone was off. He decided to pay her a visit to check in on her. No one answered when he knocked on the door three different times. Fearing the worse, he used his master key to enter Sandra's apartment. When he opened the door the apartment completely dark and the air was thick with stench as if the garbage desperately needed to be taken out. The apartment itself was also a disaster. There were sheets over all of the windows and when he turned on the lamp he saw papers strewn about. The landlord walked from room to room looking for Sandra. He approached her bathroom and found it closed and locked. He tapped on the door and made his presence known. Sandra shouted, "Don't open the door! Please, it's not safe out there!" Unsure of what was going on the landlord called 911.

Sandra was taken to the nearest emergency department for a psychiatric evaluation. When asked by the doctor why she was sleeping in her bathtub and had not left her house, Sandra stated that her house was being watched and whomever it was had slowly cornered her into her bathroom. Cameras and microphones were placed in the air vents in each room. Sandra never could figure out who it was that was monitoring her, but she felt she had gotten close to discovering an answer by analyzing the patterns she recorded over previous weeks.

Discussion. Sandra's situation reflects another example of a complex delusional system that develops slowly over time and can eventually completely take over a person's life. This example may seem pretty extreme, and it is. However, this example illustrates the possible trajectory of these types of symptoms if left untreated. Reality can become skewed and what seems extreme to most people is experienced as a perfectly rational and necessary response to an extreme event. Sandra was responding to intense fear and threat in a way that most people cannot quite imagine. However, if you could put yourself in her shoes you may begin to see how these extreme reactions *could* develop without any input or early intervention. Symptoms can hit a "plateau," in that the level of intensity and severity does not get worse; however, that does not that prevent the delusional system from further developing and expanding as more events and experiences are seen as "support." Remember, during this type of episode the brain is operating with a new system and the basis for reality has shifted such that bizarre experiences and events feel more likely to occur.

Sandra is lucky that the landlord decided to intervene and take steps toward emergency intervention. As an adult living independently, Sandra may not be around many individuals who would feel "responsible" to intervene on her behalf. However, if a coworker, friend, or family member had noticed some strange behavior and initiated a discussion earlier, Sandra may have been saved from experiencing such a scary situation.

EXHIBIT 3.4: **MICHAEL**

Michael had always been somewhat of a loner. Although he was always known to have a group of friends that he played basketball with in the evenings and accompanied to the movies and mall, his friends would generally describe him as keeping to himself. Michael would initiate plans with friends and rarely missed a group gathering. He seemed happy enough and did not appear to have any difficulty expressing his likes and dislikes, if asked. However, it was not uncommon for Michael to not say more than a few sentences during an event with friends—that was Michael, and that was how he had always been.

After high school let out in May of their junior year, Michael's friends noticed some odd behavior. Although it was not unusual for Michael to sit alone and watch from afar during a group event, his friends began to notice that he seemed distracted and was smiling to himself a lot. The strange thing is that his smiling did not seem to be associated with anything the group was discussing. Michael was often observed attending to something or someone else in the room. Interestingly, he did not seem distressed and actually seemed amused or happy. When his friends would check in with him about what he was doing or thinking, Michael would say, "Ah, nothing man, I'm good."

Michael's friends decided to leave it alone because Michael did not seem to be upset by anything in particular and did not seem to be affected in any significant ways. However, toward the end of the summer Michael's friends began to notice that he started to talk to himself. They had gotten used to the frequent smiling and attention toward some unknown person or thing. However, when they noticed that he seemed to be talking to someone who was not there they started to get worried. The dialogue was infrequent and intermittent at first, just some muttering under his breath here and there. It seemed to occur when Michael was distracted. Over time Michael was talking to himself more and more. At times he seemed to be constantly talking to someone. Luckily, Michael still did not seem to be upset by what was going on. He continued to smile and was happy to answer questions from friends and briefly participate in their conversation if asked. When friends would check in about what he was doing or whom he was talking to, Michael would always say everything was "okay" and deny that anything strange was going on.

One of Michael's friends decided to tell his own parents about Michael's behavior. He did not want to accuse Michael of anything or make him upset, and did not know what else to do. This friend's mother encouraged her son to tell Michael's mother what was going on just to be sure, and she agreed to accompany her son to Michael's house to support him during this conversation.

Discussion. This example illustrates a common course of auditory hallucinations. Fortunately for Michael he was not distressed by the experience. We can imagine that the voices he was hearing were pleasant, offering helpful or amusing comments and commentary. This is not always the case; many people experience auditory hallucinations with very negative or nasty comments and tone. Michael did not appear to have much insight into his experiences as evidenced by openly communicating with the voices in a group setting. As we have mentioned before, symptoms of psychosis are experienced as very real and are sometimes indistinguishable from reality-based experiences; they are perceived as the same. Thus, if someone has limited insight, he or she may respond to symptoms such as voices in the same way he or she would respond to any other voice. Moreover, it may be hard to distract or quiet these types of symptoms, so not engaging with them can be very difficult.

The course of Michael's auditory hallucinations reflects a characteristic development of hallucinations and other symptoms. They may start intermittently, in a more hushed tone or lower grade of intensity. Over time and without intervention, the symptoms intensify and become more prominent and harder to control. They may also become harder to distinguish from reality. It is not uncommon for hallucinations to be accompanied by a delusional belief such as an individual believing that the voice is coming from someone behind a wall or a few miles away. This type of explanation helps rationalize the experience.

Michael's friend was brave to share his concerns with his mother. Friends and peers may be some of the first to notice odd behaviors and changes. However, it can be difficult to share these concerns, as adolescents and young adults may be concerned about "snitching" and potentially being ostracized. Although Michael appears to be a calm and friendly person, his reaction may be unpredictable. Sharing the information with Michael's mother will allow the problem to be addressed in a safe manner.

CHAPTER FOUR

How Can You Intervene?

We have discussed a variety of topics related to assisting a young adult with psychosis. We have:

- Focused on building an understanding of how a young adult with psychosis might appear and behave
- Discussed the important role that early intervention can play in improving the life of a young person and the research that supports early intervention services and provides rationales that underlie this text
- Outlined in detail the symptoms of psychosis, and how they may manifest specifically in the life of a young adult
- Proposed general guidelines and considerations for interacting with a young adult in psychiatric crisis that will help guide your approach

In this chapter, we hope to build on the knowledge and the skills that you have acquired to this point and speak more specifically about assessment of safety and intervention strategies to support and assist a young adult experiencing psychosis. You now have an appreciation of how an individual experiencing psychosis may present. When considering the detailed intervention strategies that we discuss in this chapter, it is important to keep in mind a few key points:

Not every individual who is psychotic is in danger/dangerous: Although we strongly encourage a "better safe than sorry" approach, it should be noted that the majority of individuals with psychosis are not dangerous to themselves or others. There are many individuals who experience psychosis on some level who elect not to participate in treatment and live safe lives despite their symptoms. Moreover, individuals may demonstrate aggressiveness and have no evidence or risk of psychosis. In this chapter, we discuss risk and danger and will approach these topics conservatively. However, we do not want this conservative approach to reinforce the stigmatization of individuals with psychosis as dangerous.

Not every person behaving strangely is psychotic: By this point, you understand that psychosis consists of more than simply unusual behavior; it is a constellation of particular symptoms that impair an individual's ability to interact with reality and function normally. There are a variety of reasons that someone might behave in a way that seems unusual, including intoxication from drugs or alcohol, eccentric personality characteristics, or other mental health concerns. It is important not to assume that an individual is psychotic simply because he or she behaves in an unusual way.

Not all situations in which you may be able to assist will be an acute crisis: Through our discussions in this chapter, we sometimes focus on the more extreme or urgent situations; this is because these situations often require more complicated assessment and intervention. It is possible, even likely, that the situation in which you feel compelled to offer your assistance is largely unremarkable. That is, there is no immediate concern about danger. Young adults with psychosis may present in a variety of ways. Some will present with behaviors that are difficult to ignore and are even potentially dangerous. Others may isolate themselves, demonstrate changes in work or school performance, and other less subtle changes in behavior.

We begin this chapter with a guided tour of how to assess a variety of factors, including safety, that will be critical for the interaction. These assessment opportunities will assist in preparing to intervene, and inform if, when, and how to intervene. Following that, we outline a set of steps in order to guide you in having a safe and supportive interaction with the individual you are assisting. We also discuss possible responses from the young adult and provide a flow chart to aid in decision making. Although we believe that many of the suggestions we have made (and will make) would be useful in a variety of situations in which someone may need psychiatric assistance, it is important to be mindful that the strategies suggested have been developed with the needs of a young adult experiencing psychosis in mind, and may not translate seamlessly to other situations. Exhibits 4.1 to 4.6 provide some fictional examples of scenarios that may be of help.

ASSESSMENT OF AN OBJECTIVE CONCERN: IS THERE A PROBLEM?

If you are considering assisting a young adult in psychiatric crisis, there is something about the person or the situation that has piqued your concern. In order to organize your efforts and understand how you can best be of help, it is important to take a few moments to examine your specific concerns about the situation. This will help begin to formulate a plan for approach, if necessary. What grabbed your attention? When considering if there is a problem and what the problem might be, we suggest paying attention to your internal cues. That is, mentally inventory the situation and make note of which aspects make you feel uneasy. Trust your judgment. If a situation concerns you, it is likely that your assistance will be valuable.

By this point, you have a certain amount of knowledge about the types of behaviors that might indicate psychosis (e.g., drastic changes in functioning, responding to internal stimuli); in this section, we discuss specific types of behavior that we recommend you to consider as part of your assessment of the situation. We discuss a variety of unsafe or bizarre behaviors, as well as general "red flags" that may be an indication that a young person is in a psychiatric crisis.

Unsafe or Bizarre Behaviors

As we have discussed, the symptoms of psychosis may lead to a young person behaving in unsafe or seemingly bizarre ways. It is not hard to imagine why these behaviors often become a source of concern. In many cases, they are the "tipping point" that indicates to others that the person is in need of immediate assistance. These behaviors can take a number of forms; we discuss several, but there are innumerable options for the way bizarre and concerning behaviors may manifest.

FEAR OR SENSE OF THREAT

It is not uncommon for individuals with a paranoid ideation to feel fearful or threatened by any situations that others perceive as benign. This fear or sense of threat that a person experiences warrants an attempt at providing assistance. In some cases, a person may present as obviously fearful and eager for assistance. For example, a person feels that her roommates are trying to poison her, and she is scared to return home. This allows a perfect opportunity for intervention when you can offer to assist someone in feeling safer. Individuals having experiences similar to this are likely to appear sullen, withdrawn, and overly anxious. They may be reluctant to discuss their concerns overtly, particularly if their fear is more general and they are not sure whom they can trust.

Alternatively, some young people may respond to feelings of paranoia with anger, a feeling that they need to defend themselves, or notions of revenging the wrongs that have been done to them. For instance, a person may express that he is sure that his neighbor is stealing his belongings at night, and plans to sit up all night waiting at the door with a gun in case the neighbor comes in. In this scenario, the neighbor may be in danger, but any number of other people may also be in danger if the person interprets them to be trying to get into his home. This is clearly a more troubling and urgent scenario. Nonetheless, it is important to remember that in the perception of this individual, he is indeed being threatened, and to him, the response is appropriate. Although this certainly does not excuse such behavior, it does provide us with a lens for understanding and empathizing with the person. On a more subtle scale, if you notice that a person appears to be "hiding" in the back of a class or appears uneasy with eyes darting back and forth across the room, it may indicate that he or she is having a troubling experience that may benefit from help and support. If you have observed similar fear or sense of threat in an adolescent or young adult, then assistance is prudent.

GRANDIOSITY

It is not uncommon for young adults with psychosis to experience grandiosity, whether as a facet of their delusional system, or as a result of manic mood disturbance. Grandiosity may manifest in a variety of ways. For some individuals, it may present as the development of an overly important sense of self that is a departure from their normal behavior. This may result in a resistance to authority, a sense of entitlement, a belief that others are greatly envious, and an agitated reaction to any indication that their beliefs may not be true. Individuals experiencing this type of grandiosity are likely to strain interpersonal relationships with their behaviors.

Alternatively, grandiosity may be more driven by delusional content; for instance, the belief that an individual is a religious, royal, or leadership figure or that he or she is related to such a person. It is not difficult to imagine how such a belief may result in bizarre behavior. In some cases, such individuals may be found preaching in public spaces or attempting to distribute orders to their believed followers. They may fail to respect laws or regulations, believing that they are above them. If they believe that they are related to or have a relationship with an important person, they may be at risk of stalking or harassing the person. Not surprisingly, this can result in a number of problems including contact with law enforcement.

Furthermore, young people who experience grandiose symptoms may also believe that they have special powers such as the ability to control the behavior of others, or invincibility. Such beliefs may lead the person to engage in risky and potentially dangerous behavior believing that they will not suffer consequences. If you notice or perceive these types of behaviors and develop concern about the rationality or thought process of the person, intervention is certainly warranted.

DANGEROUSNESS

As we have discussed, the symptoms of psychosis may lead to a number of unusual behaviors. Those that could put the individual or others at risk of harm are most concerning. These dangerous behaviors may take a number of different forms. In general, any concern about dangerous behavior would benefit from some level of intervention.

For instance, in some cases, the intent to harm oneself or another may be explicitly stated and seemingly intentional. If, for instance, a young person believes that a neighbor is trying to kill her, she may announce that the next time she sees the neighbor, she will act first. Or, an individual experiencing a delusion that he is a religious figure might express that he plans to sacrifice himself in order to save mankind. Such unambiguous expressions of plans to harm create little doubt that intervention is necessary.

In other cases, the danger may be less intentional and more haphazard. This may be a combination of acting on delusional beliefs, lack of ability to think through consequences due to disorganization, or compromised judgment; for example, a young adult who is scaling a water tower in order to better control the daily activities of town residents, or someone who is attempting to swim across a lake in order to confuse the location devices believed to be implanted in his or her skin. These acts are qualitatively different than those described earlier; however, they too are a cause for concern. These behaviors do not carry the intent to harm, but it is not difficult to imagine that harm could easily occur, and in some situations others may be placed at risk as well.

Some behaviors may be even less obviously dangerous, for instance, a person inappropriately dressed for the weather. Imagine a young person with psychosis wearing a parka on a hot summer day, or conversely, heading out for a walk during a snowstorm without a coat. These seemingly eccentric or absentminded behaviors can result in serious consequences and should be considered as concerning as more overt dangerous behavior.

HYPERSEXUALITY

A relatively common pattern of bizarre behavior involves an element of hypersexuality. This refers to an individual engaging in overly sexualized behavior in an inappropriate setting or context. These behaviors may be the result of a manic state, with sexual behavior exhibiting a euphoric element and fueled by excessive energy. For instance, someone may begin dancing in a sexually explicit manner while at a family gathering where music is playing, or a person may disrobe in inappropriate places in order to gain the sexual attention of others.

In other cases, hypersexual behavior may be the result of grossly disorganized behavior in which the person is not able to "filter" his or her sexual impulses to conform to culturally appropriate norms. For example, individuals who are extremely disorganized may begin masturbating at the sight of someone they find attractive, whether it is in the public library or the privacy of their home. Others may hear voices commanding them to exhibit sexually explicit behaviors and feel powerless to resist.

These behaviors, while obviously upsetting to others who may be nearby, are also potentially dangerous for the individual engaging in them. Hypersexual behavior may increase a person's vulnerability to be victimized when such behaviors gain the attention of potential predators. In addition, although it is unlikely that the intent of the person is to violate laws, many hypersexual behaviors can cross boundaries into illegality. For example, disrobing in public, urinating in public, or impulsively touching other people could all result in criminal charges, and in many states could result in the young person being registered as a sex offender for many years.

General "Red Flags"

Not all behaviors that indicate a need for intervention are acutely unsafe. As we discussed in the section "How Do Symptoms Appear in Daily Life?" in Chapter 2, there are a number of behavioral changes that frequently occur when a person is experiencing psychosis that are likely to draw attention and raise concern but are not necessarily unsafe. These behaviors are briefly reviewed here in regard to their relationship to the assessment of objective concern; however, they are discussed in greater detail in Chapter 2, which may be helpful to review as you consider your concerns. Keep in mind that these changes may occur rather suddenly or more gradually over time. So, having knowledge of the person over time is likely to be helpful in understanding whether the behaviors are normal *for that person*. We suggest trusting your judgment if you start to feel that the following behaviors may be indicative of a larger issue.

CHANGES IN FUNCTIONAL ABILITIES

Individuals experiencing psychosis often demonstrate a decline in their ability to function under the demands of day-to-day life. For instance, an individual may begin to demonstrate impairment in self-care, such as hygiene or grooming. A young person who was previously fashion and image conscious may now bathe infrequently, appear unkempt, wear dirty clothes, or have a general apathy about his or her appearance. He or she may also have drastic changes in eating or sleeping, which, onto themselves, may also be evidence of a problem. Such changes in functioning are likely to cause particular concern when they appear together. That is, a young person begins refusing to eat and also demonstrating a notable change in hygiene. It should also be noted that any person may experience such changes from time to time on a short-term basis. For example, during a period of particular stress, like finals week in college, a young person may have notable changes in hygiene, sleep, or eating; however, once the period of stress has resolved, these will likely return to normal. For individuals experiencing psychosis, these changes are likely to remain static until an intervention occurs. If you are unsure whether the changes you are observing are transient or static, consider the presence of other concerning behaviors mentioned in this chapter. It is likely that a person will exhibit more than one concerning behavior.

CHANGES IN SCHOOL OR WORK PERFORMANCE

Similar to changes in functional abilities, changes in work or school performance may be evidence of transient stress. Many young people fail the occasional examination, get behind on coursework, or are less than reliable employees from time to time. However, a consistent change in these behaviors may be evidence of a greater problem. Often these changes are accompanied by other, unusual behaviors that may help you to determine whether you are observing a normal variation in behavior or a concerning change. For instance, a formerly reliable, punctual employee who has been more than an hour late for his shift for the last 2 weeks is looking unkempt and is making frequent errors on tasks that he previously had mastered.

SELF-DIALOGUING OR RESPONDING TO INTERNAL STIMULI

These behaviors tend to be regarded as universally unusual, and are likely to draw your attention. Although many of us may mutter to ourselves while in deep concentration, or laugh at a silly memory that pops into our head, we are able to realign our focus with the physical world relatively quickly. People experiencing hallucinations may not be able to do this. Their internal and external stimuli may be equally strong and demanding of their attention. They are likely to appear distracted, even if you are trying to engage them in conversation, or, when alone, may be observed behaving in ways that appear as if they are in a conversation.

SOCIAL ISOLATION

Again, this is a "red flag" that likely needs to be considered in context. Some people simply have a preference for spending time alone, and this is not necessarily a problem. However, if a previously outgoing or social person begins to express a strong preference for avoiding people, there may be a reason for concern—particularly if this occurs in the presence of any of the other "red flags" discussed.

Taken together, the recipe for a successful interaction includes a well-informed idea about what prompted your concern in the first place. This information will be important as you develop your plan for how to approach the person and decide exactly what to say. Moreover, this information and assessment of objective concern will likely be helpful at later stages in which the individual engages with treatment. You may be asked to share what it was that prompted you to intervene. Because early intervention for psychosis is critical, understanding the development and progression of difficulty will substantiate the need for treatment in the earliest stages rather than assuming that the behavior is better explained by some other issue.

SYSTEMATIC ASSESSMENT OF THE ENVIRONMENT: WHEN AND HOW SHOULD I INTERVENE?

Assessment of the Situation

When entering a situation where a young adult is in psychiatric crisis, a systematic assessment of the situation is needed in order to evaluate safety and take note of importance pieces of information. This assessment considers the notable features of the person and situation, safety of the environment and situation, your own safety, and the safety of the young adult in crisis.

Before you begin considering how you might intervene in the situation at hand, you may want to take careful stock of the features of the situation. These are details that may be important in later steps in the process. First, take note of the location. If you are in an unfamiliar location, make note of landmarks or notable features nearby. This information will be helpful if you need to direct responders to you. Second, make note of the physical appearance of the individual you are hoping to assist. What is the person wearing? Are you able to approximate his or her race or ethnicity? Height? Is there anything distinctive about his or her appearance? What about the way he or she moves? Next, pay attention to the behavior and words of the person. Is the person saying anything specific? If so, it will be helpful to remember this if possible. Make note of any behaviors that stand out to you as odd in the situational context. For example, running, dancing, hiding, or posturing in an aggressive manner would all be notable behaviors.

Next, we ask you to consider the environment and the situation in which you are attempting to insert yourself. Is the environment a safe one? There are a variety of environmental factors that may make it unsafe to approach an individual. For instance, if a young adult is in the middle of a busy street behaving bizarrely, he or she could likely benefit from some assistance; however, the situation will put you in danger if you attempt to approach the person. Or if the individual is in a physical altercation with another person, it is likely unsafe to directly intervene. In these cases, the safety of the young adult is also a primary concern. In situations where an individual needs assistance, but it is unsafe for you to approach, emergency service intervention is necessary and will help to support the safety of all parties.

In addition to environmental dangers, there may be other circumstances that would cause the situation to be too dangerous to engage. In some cases, the individual may be potentially dangerous to you if you approach. For instance, a person may state an explicit threat ("If you come closer, I will …"); such statements should be taken seriously and you should not try to handle this situation without the help of emergency services. Additionally, take note if the individual has anything that could potentially be used as a weapon. This could be something obvious, such as a knife, but it also might include something heavy that could be thrown, such as a chair or a rock. If the individual is not willing to step away from the potential weapon, it is best to allow emergency responders to handle this situation.

As a "take-home message," we suggest that you consider your safety first. Do not put yourself in danger in order to assist a young adult in crisis. Consider the metaphor of the oxygen masks on an airplane: You are instructed to secure your own mask before assisting others. Without ensuring your own safety, you will not be able to help others in the way you hoped.

Assessment of the Person's Safety

Although a formal and thorough assessment of safety should be left to a qualified mental health professional, a simplified assessment of the person's ability to stay safe may help you to determine what actions might be the most helpful. Put simply, your goal in assessing the individual's safety should be to determine whether or not you need to call emergency services immediately, or not. If you receive an indication that the person is not able to stay safe, either through his or her verbal responses or his or her behavior, you should call emergency services immediately in order to have the person evaluated.

As you have assessed the situation per the previous step, you have probably gathered some information about whether the situation is safe for the individual. It is likely that if you have determined that it is unsafe for you to approach the person, then for one reason or another it is also unsafe for that person—for instance, if he or she is climbing a water tower, or standing in the middle of a busy road. These are clearly situations in which the person's safety is compromised. Additionally, you will want to consider whether it appears that the person is at risk of hurting himself or herself or someone else—for instance, if he or she has a weapon or is expressing threats to do either. In these cases, we encourage you to involve emergency services as your method of intervening. Do not enter the situation yourself. Instead, you may be most helpful by staying on the phone with the dispatcher to provide continuing information about the person's behavior or whereabouts.

Provided you have determined that it is safe to approach the person, you may have an opportunity to continue to gather information about safety throughout the interaction. If the person appears fearful, it may seem appropriate to begin with questions about safety. After all, if he or she is feeling fearful, safety is on his or her mind too. In other cases, it may be more effective to spend a few minutes discussing less intimidating subjects. Even seemingly, mundane questions like "How is your day going?" can start to elicit information about the person's state of mind and safety.

Even some nonspecific information about the person's safety can help you to determine the level of urgency with which you need to respond. Consider the following suggestions as ways to begin a conversation about safety.

You seem worried; is there anything I can do to help?

Do you feel safe?

Is there something you are afraid of?

I'd like to help you feel safer; is there something I can do?

Is there someone I could call to help you feel safer?

It seems like you're feeling pretty angry. Is there anything in particular upsetting you?

Such phrasings introduce the notion of safety but allow the individuals you are assisting to be in control of the situation. You are asking for their active participation in understanding their concerns. Ideally, their responses will also help you to develop a plan of action to help them feel safe and determine next steps to help them access mental health services.

Direct discussion of safety can feel awkward and intrusive. You will sometimes need to ask questions or discuss topics that you might otherwise shy away from in daily conversation. However, if you feel that there is a need to be concerned about safety, we strongly encourage you not to shy away from the subject entirely. If you are unable to determine whether you need to call 911 from the less direct methods suggested previously, consider a more direct approach. Some individuals with psychosis may respond more coherently to direct and simplistic questions. This often means that such questions lack the "finesse" of how we might usually talk about sensitive topics. Consider the following direct questions about safety.

Do you feel like hurting someone?

Do you feel like you want to end your life?

Are you having thoughts about not being alive anymore?

In some cases, particularly if the person is experiencing symptoms of disorganization, the person may have difficulty articulating whether he or she feels safe and what you might be able to do to help. There may be many "I don't know" responses. This may not be an avoidance of the questions you are asking, but rather may be a product of the person's disorganized thought process—he or she genuinely may not know. Despite your best efforts, there may still be situations in which the person you are assisting is not able or willing to discuss safety concerns. In such circumstances, we suggest that you consider two sets of information:

1. *The evidence of the situation.* Review the safety information about the situation and the surrounding facts.
   - Is the person in immediate physical danger?
   - Does he or she have a weapon or access to one?
   - Is the person making verbal threats to harm himself or herself or someone else?
2. *Your "gut" feeling*
   - Do you have reason to believe that the person is being dishonest?
   - Is the person is too confused to understand questions or respond appropriately?
   - Are you concerned that the person may be unable to complete basic tasks to ensure safety?

If any of these are true, it is best that the person see a mental health professional for evaluation as soon as possible. Concern about immediate threat or harm, or difficulty expressing safety necessitates a call to 911. If you have access to a mental health professional—for instance, an on-campus counseling center or a counselor within a medical office, or if you happen to have contact information for the young adult's therapist—it may be possible to seek consultation from this person in order to guide your decisions, *in addition to* a call to 911. As previously discussed, it will be most helpful to stay on the line with responders until they arrive.

If, after reviewing the facts, you have decided that the person is not in immediate danger, but you continue to feel uneasy, it may be helpful to reach out to someone close to the individual who knows him or her better and might be able to provide support in staying safe. This may mean offering to call a parent, friend, sibling, or provider if the person is willing to let you do that. Also, at this point, you will have the opportunity to initiate a conversation about the possibility of receiving help and to begin to build a collaborative plan in which you can assist the person. These and other steps are discussed later in this chapter.

INTRODUCING AND ENCOURAGING THE IDEA OF HELP: WHAT CAN I DO?

If you are able to determine that safety is not an immediate concern and the identified person does not appear to be at risk to harm himself or herself or someone else, there are a number of methods of introducing the notion of treatment and engaging in care. Chapter 3 described important considerations when introducing this discussion and critical verbal and nonverbal factors that will contribute to a more successful interaction. Thus, Chapter 3 outlined the "how" in preparing for this type of interaction. Conversely, we now focus on the "what" factors when the situation is underway. As we have described, the first step is assessment of safety and we provided several considerations and questions for how to assess safety and make a determination about immediate, emergency intervention. This initial dialogue may or may not include discussion of the observed symptoms or behaviors that were the initial cause for concern. In the next sections, we describe how you can initiate an empathic conversation about observed symptoms and behaviors, assuming safety concerns have been ruled out.

It is important to acknowledge from the start that the person displaying concerning behavior may not agree to talk to you, at any level. He or she may not answer your questions about safety, agree to meet with you to discuss your concerns, or engage in any conversation at all. Thus, it may be necessary to make a decision based on little information. This is why the "better safe than sorry" approach is so important. However, even if individuals are initially agreeable to meet with you or have a seemingly harmless conversation, their demeanor may quickly shift for a number of reasons such as discomfort about discussing personal information, or paranoia. Again, you may be required to make a decision with very little collaboration or input from the individual. If the person has refused to speak with you but is deemed safe, then the best you can hope for is another opportunity to have the conversation at a later date. However, if you felt that safety was a concern then emergency contacts should be made. The next subsections are presented with the assumption that the individual is participating in an interaction with you at some level, even minimally.

Step 1: Create a Supportive Environment

The first step is to create a supportive environment. In general, you want to provide a space that allows for privacy and safety, if possible. This may mean that you ask this individual where he or she would like to meet, or provide a space that meets these goals. If you are able to collaborate on a space or environment, it is always helpful as it facilitates rapport and commitment to the interaction. It is best to initiate a conversation as quickly as possible if you have the individual's interest and collaboration.

A supportive environment is not just about the physical space, but also the interpersonal tone and "vibe." Thus, you may not find the perfect spot to initiate a conversation and that is okay. If it is easy and feasible, pursue it. If, however, it will delay an important conversation, then do your best to create a supportive environment with verbal and nonverbal factors. Consider discussing less "heavy" or serious topics before delving into your concerns. Nonthreatening topics like sports, the weather, or observations of the environment ("That fountain is so calming and pretty") may be options for less serious conversation.

Step 2: Initiating the Conversation

At this point, you will have already asked questions related to safety. Thus, you may find yourself reiterating some of the points brought up in the initial stages of the conversation. However, here the goal is to reflect on the reason for your approach and concern as opposed to gathering information. As we have mentioned, individuals in psychiatric crisis, and particularly those experiencing psychosis, are very vulnerable for a number of reasons. Vulnerability is primarily related to difficulties differentiating symptoms from reality, and feeling a lack of control of symptoms and experiences. These two factors, as well as others, are likely to impact how a person receives your questions and concerns. The best approach, as stated previously in the "Verbal Behavior" section of Chapter 3, is simple and direct questions and statements. We recommend statements such as the following:

> I have noticed that you seem very distressed and distracted, and I would like to help you.
>
> What you wrote in your history paper really made me worried.
>
> You've been sitting in the back of the room a lot. You seem scared.
>
> You seem anxious or afraid.
>
> I heard you talking to yourself in the bedroom when no one else was there.

In addition, we recommend open and closed questions similar to the examples that follow:

> Who or what is bothering you?
>
> You seem [anxious, scared, worried]. What is on your mind?

Are you feeling confused about anything?

Are you hearing something that I can't hear?

You will notice that some of these questions and statements are asking about the same information in different ways. Some are more direct, and some are more vague. There is no one "right way" to introduce these difficult questions and statements. At times, individuals may feel very overwhelmed by a question or statement about voices if they have not shared this experience with anyone. However, some individuals may feel relieved that someone noticed and started the conversation for them so they did not have to. Based on the setting, established relationships, and the nature of the symptoms and circumstances, a more or less direct approach may be beneficial. Unfortunately, you may not have much information about how a person will receive your attempt at help. Just do your best at demonstrating interest, understanding, and a desire to help. Follow the person's lead and attend to his or her responses. You may find that certain types of questions work better than others with a given person. For instance, one person may be limited to brief responses, so yes/no questions may work best, while another person may be able to respond with more detail if prompted by questions that cannot be answered with a "yes" or a "no."

Step 3: Introducing the Notion of Treatment or Help

After you have determined that safety is not an immediate concern and started a dialogue about the symptoms and behaviors of concern, it is time to begin to discuss steps toward an intervention plan. First, it is important to discuss the general benefits of treatment and what it may entail. Some individuals may have prior experience with psychiatric treatment in some form, but others may not. Thus, describing the ways that treatment can be helpful is important. This description does not need to be highly detailed; there are a few basic pieces of information to get across to provide an initial and general understanding. You may decide to emphasize some information more than others given the nature of the situation, the identified symptoms and behaviors, and what areas of distress, if any, the person has shared with you. Remember that for many young adults experiencing psychosis, they perceive the world around them as having changed, rather than identifying a change in their own thoughts and behaviors. For this reason, it is important to emphasize the things that *they* perceive as the problem and how treatment may help them with that. Some brief examples are provided as follows.

> Sometimes people find it helpful to talk to someone about strange or troubling experiences and there are professionals who specialize in this type of thing.

> You mentioned that someone may be following you. Talking to a therapist or doctor may help you understand why this is happening and what it may mean.

> Have you ever heard of therapists or counselors? They help people understand and cope with difficult situations and experiences. This might be helpful with what you are going through. They may also be able to help you work through this disagreement you had with Professor XX.

> I've known a lot of people who have had problems at work from time to time. Some of them have found it helpful to talk to a therapist about stress at work. Would that be something that might be helpful for you?

Identified individuals may have a variety of reactions and responses to your attempts at discussing their experiences. These are likely to directly impact the approach you choose and to determine what paths to treatment are most feasible. Similar to the examples of statements and inquiries described earlier for discussing concerning symptoms and behaviors, your ideas and plans for engagement with treatment should also be simple and direct. Although we certainly do not encourage dishonesty or coercion, declarative statements are likely to be most effective. If asked, it is likely that most individuals will say "no" to an immediate treatment response or plan. However, stating that a plan will be initiated in some way is more likely to support a collaborative approach in determining which plan or path is selected. Moreover, highlighting the importance of their input will be critical. See some examples are as follows:

> I am worried about you. Let's develop a plan to get you some help.

> Together, let's figure out how to get you feeling better.

> There are many ways to help you with this problem. Let's find one that works best for you.

Once it has been established that a plan will be developed, introduce a variety of options. Again, the goal is engagement with treatment or creation of a plan that will eventually lead to treatment. Collaboration is critical to this process and that may mean compromising for a less preferred path, as long as it is a path. We encourage you to be knowledgeable about the various treatment options or paths appropriate for your setting, circumstance, and access. It is important to identify all options before pursuing any specific strategy so that the process continues to be collaborative while also being as comprehensive and thorough as possible. Writing down the various options is often helpful to maintain focus, compare various options, and generally present all the options available. Moreover, this helps to establish that a plan is being generated rather than more of a hypothetical scenario. Writing information down will also assist the person in following your conversation, which may be challenging depending on the severity of symptoms the person is experiencing.

First, inquire about family members and/or trusted supports who may want to be part of the discussion and/or development of a path toward treatment. Ask about local individuals who can meet you immediately, and nonlocal individuals who may be available by phone. This is particularly important if you do not have an established relationship with the individual. Having a trusted family member or friend as part of the process will greatly facilitate effectiveness and better ensure commitment to an identified plan. If the individual is a minor, contacting parents, caregivers, or guardians should be a goal, if possible, in all situations. If trusted individuals in the person's life have been identified, attempt to contact them immediately so that they can be present and/or involved as soon as possible. These individuals are likely to be very important in any future steps that are identified or initiated. Second, inquire about treatment that is already ongoing. If someone already has a provider, introduce the option to contact the provider or providers. Record the name and contact information of the treatment provider so that the individual, you, or someone else along the treatment path may contact the provider. Offer to assist with making phone calls. Some people may find it overwhelming to have a conversation with someone about the difficulties they are having. They may prefer to have you speak, or to share the conversation in a particular way.

If it has been determined that there is no ongoing treatment, then it may be helpful to briefly discuss different types of treatment options that may be pursued at that time. The ideal outcome is that an appointment or concrete connection with a treatment provider can be made while you are sitting with the individual. That is why it is important to be familiar with treatment resources if you feel that you may be in a position to intervene during a psychiatric crisis. Any hesitation or delay in identifying resources may disrupt momentum toward selecting and committing to a treatment option or plan. Options and resources that should be introduced include the campus-counseling center and/or other outpatient treatment options, guidance counselors, primary care or family doctors, and a hospital evaluation and/or inpatient admission. These options are likely to be unfamiliar and perceived as scary, intrusive, or not applicable. At this time, it may be important to reiterate the general benefits of treatment. Once several options have been identified, ask the individual to select the options he or she would like to pursue. Again, declarative statements are helpful in establishing that a plan will be pursued. The path to treatment may include following up with several of these options in a sequential or concurrent approach rather than picking just one. However, the individual may only be agreeable to selecting one. If that is the case, remember that collaboration increases the likelihood that the person will adhere to the plan and follow his or her initial preference. Keep the *person's* goals in mind, and understand that while emphasizing your own agenda (getting the person treatment) is tempting, it may actually backfire. Be prepared to compromise. If the person is willing to do only one of the many things you suggest, accept that and encourage follow-through with that one item.

You may find that, while agreeable, an individual may not be able to participate in this kind of process for a number of reasons such as severe symptoms, drug or alcohol intoxication, or cognitive impairment. You may have to make a determination on your own. The goal is always pursuing a link to care. If the person is too ill to participate, then an emergency intervention is most appropriate.

DEVELOPING A PLAN

Now that you have an option or a number of options to pursue, the next step is to identify the steps needed to implement the different treatment options. Collaboration facilitates this as individuals are more likely to commit to a treatment plan if they had a hand in developing it. For example, individuals may say that they would like to contact their pediatrician first, a person they have known for years and trust. However, they may be open to also contacting the guidance counselor at their school for an initial appointment after checking in with the pediatrician. On the other hand, some individuals may be willing to contact only their parents/caregiver/

guardian and no one else, or will only agree to leaving a message for the campus-counseling center. We consider any level of agreement a success, even if an alternative plan with more assurances was available. As you might expect with anyone in need of treatment, successfully engaging with treatment requires "buy-in" and motivation.

Before we guide you through the steps of developing a plan toward treatment engagement, we would like to share some important considerations that will support success. First and foremost, resist the urge to challenge a rationale for a strategy or "force" a plan. As we have mentioned before, it may be true that you know what is *best* with regard to a sound plan and even have better insight into the issues that are present, but the goal is to increase the likelihood that a plan is actually carried out. Therefore, if an individual agrees to see make an appointment with the school guidance counselor for a perceived issue with "anxiety" or "sleep," that is just fine. The goal of the interaction is not to get agreement about what symptoms and experiences are present, but to engage with a provider who can have this discussion on a more long-term basis. Second, we believe that your aim should be to facilitate a step toward treatment. That step may only be a discussion of treatment, with no agreement from the individual to do anything. If there is no concern about safety, that may be all you get, and that is still a step! Forcing a plan (outside of emergency intervention) is nearly guaranteed to be ignored. Instead, we believe that even the most basic plan, if developed collaboratively, will have more success facilitating engagement with treatment in the short and long term.

As a first step in the plan, make all of the contacts that you have agreed on. This may include a call to a family member or friend, but can also include calling a clinic or mental health professional. You may have to leave messages and that is okay. Again, making contact of any form is the goal, even if the response is not immediate. Messages should include the name and contact information for the individual, at a minimum. Leaving other detailed, personal information is not necessary in the initial message. If the individual feels comfortable, he or she may also decide to share a few details about the current situation. It may help to practice what will be left on the message and what to say when the call is returned. Developing a script can be helpful to decrease anxiety about discussing the situation at a later date. An individual may decide to develop a script but is not ready to make a call. In this situation, sharing the script with a family member or friend can also be helpful in the event that the family member or friend makes the call to a provider or is present to assist the individual at a later date. Moreover, if the individual is a minor it may be more appropriate for a parent or guardian to speak to a mental health provider. Following are some example scripts that may be useful.

> Hi, my name is XX. I am calling to make an appointment to discuss some trouble I've had recently. I can be reached at the following number...
>
> Hello, my name is XX. I would like to make an appointment with one of your clinicians. I can be reached at the following number...

Second, be prepared to assist in the development of a plan for the immediate future, for the next several hours as well as the next several days. Depending on the situation, it may be difficult to connect with treatment or a treatment provider during the interaction, and often appointments are scheduled several days or weeks out. Thus, developing a detailed plan for the immediate future until the contact can be made is important. Moreover, a detailed plan regarding the days and hours leading up to the scheduled contact is also important so that the path to treatment does not lose momentum or dissolve during a period of ambiguity. We encourage you to write down the plans for the next few hours as well as the next few days so that both of you can follow along, identify any discrepancies, and ensure that all steps are covered. If the individual is unable to do this and a family member or trusted friend is present, follow the same procedure with him or her. Expectations for the immediate future may also include discussion of return to school, work, or other obligations. Depending on the circumstances leading to this encounter and severity of symptoms present, it may be more important for the individual to stay home where less stress is likely to be present. We have included a generic form that may be used as a model or example for building such a plan (see Exhibit 4.7).

Discussion of additional options or alternatives may also be appropriate to supplement identified steps. These include reviewing procedures for contacting emergency organizations such as 911 or local crisis-based intervention programs. It may also be helpful to provide information about 24-hour hotlines to call for help in the event the individual does become more distressed and is ready to seek treatment on his or her own. We encourage all individuals, groups, and organizations reading this to develop a brochure or pamphlet with these numbers for easy distribution. This streamlines the presentation of these numbers and reduces delay. Many hotlines and crisis response organizations have wallet-sized cards with their information on them, and are happy to provide them free of charge to people who would like to distribute them. Having such information at hand formalizes the treatment engagement procedure, and a having a formal procedure in place also normalizes the situation and sends the message that a strategy is already in place because this is something that happens to people from time to time.

More often than not, we expect that the interactions you facilitate will be brief and specific. However, you may have the opportunity to have a lengthier and more detailed conversation and plan. If the latter is the case, we would also like to introduce some additional considerations that may be helpful to address. The following conversations may not be possible for most individuals in crisis for a number of reasons, some of which are anxiety, feeling overwhelmed by the situation and / or symptoms, or any number of reasons. However, if possible, it may be helpful to identify and troubleshoot barriers to carrying out the specified plan. Barriers include obstacles that will delay or affect carrying out any steps in the plan, such as transportation problems, financial problems, or conflicting obligations. It may also be helpful to acknowledge that the individual may change his or her mind about carrying out the plan, or others may feel the plan is not necessary and try to talk the individual out of it. Consider the following examples:

> I'm happy to hear that you are looking forward to your appointment in a couple weeks. It seems like our conversation has been helpful. I wonder if there is anything that could stand in the way of getting you to the appointment such as work or upcoming school assignments.

> I know you went back and forth about leaving a message for the counselor. If you start to change your mind before the appointment, what can you tell yourself to remind you why this is important?

> I'm happy we were able to develop a plan together. Would it be helpful to discuss some other details such as how to get to the appointment?

Again, it may be helpful to highlight that these situations can occur, and problem solve around these barriers so that the plan can continue to be carried out. Use your judgment as to whether this type of conversation will be helpful rather than confusing. If the individual you are assisting has already introduced concerns about carrying out the plan, and is able to demonstrate some reasoning ability, then this may be helpful. If, however, you are already having trouble establishing a plan in any form, this lengthier discussion may be too confusing.

COMMON REACTIONS AND RESPONSES

We have led you through the steps in facilitating an interaction and hopefully engagement with a plan for accessing treatment. While we have introduced some common reactions at each stage, we believe it is important to revisit the range of reactions and responses that may come up. These reactions are not meant to dissuade you from helping but instead to be prepared to navigate different types of reactions. In general, a "successful" interaction is a broad notion comprising many different types of outcomes. Success can mean an appointment for one person, or the consideration of an appointment for another.

First and foremost, it is important to recognize that you may hear "no" right from the start: "no" meeting, "no" conversation, and just plain "no." Unfortunately, this is a very likely response from someone experiencing the overwhelming, confusing, and potentially scary symptoms of psychosis. Bringing another individual into the mix may feel completely unbearable, and so involving supportive others might not be an option either. Moreover, it may be perceived that acknowledging or discussing symptoms will make them worse in a number of ways; so status quo, although uncomfortable and upsetting, may be preferable. In this situation, your best bet is to make it known that you are available for support, to lend an ear, or to assist in seeking help if the individual ever feels it is needed. You may also consider asking if you can check in from time to time, if appropriate. Unless you are concerned about immediate safety, then this will be where your interaction ends. Although you may not feel that you made any headway, you planted a seed and that is certainly important.

Hopefully, the individual is willing to engage with you in some way. If so, the responses at each stage we have discussed can vary. Chapter 3 described in detail different types of reactions and responses that may be present and why they may arise. Remember that the individual you are trying to help is also trying to develop some understanding of what is happening, and is likely still trying to make sense of everything he or she is experiencing. You may find that someone is willing and interested in having a conversation about "distress" or "difficulty" but may become scared or agitated when questions about symptoms or problem behaviors are introduced. Moreover, some may be willing to talk about their experiences but become very angry when the notion of needing "help" is introduced. Paranoia is very likely for individuals with delusions—if you are asking questions, then you may be "involved."

Unfortunately, the most predictable part of this process is unpredictability. There will be a lot that you do not know and cannot know (e.g., illness and otherwise) that may affect how someone responds to this type of interaction or conversation. We encourage you to be knowledge-able about the verbal and nonverbal factors that will be beneficial in every situation, no matter the individual differences. These factors will set and maintain a tone and vibe that will demonstrate support, nonjudgment, and a desire to help.

HOW TO DETERMINE IMMEDIATE NEEDS

Although previous chapters aimed to encourage and prepare profession-als to intervene, the current chapter seeks to provide the tools to engage a person who appears at risk and to facilitate connection with some form of treatment. We have also provided detailed information about reactions and responses that may present challenges to coordinating engagement with treatment.

Thus, this chapter has provided the nuts and bolts of employing the "better safe than sorry" approach. Now that you have the information, we would like to guide you through a strategy to implement the approach we have been discussing, including considerations that will greatly inform the route of treatment engagement.

Figure 4.1 illustrates a decision tree to guide you through the inter-action, highlighting critical factors along the way. Given the plethora of information that we have provided up this point, this may seem like a very basic illustration of the important decisions we are encouraging you to make. However, this model is simple by design for two important reasons.

First, because such situations are so varied it is impossible to develop a model or guide that can account for every scenario. There will always be outliers, unique characteristics, and individual differences. Second, while the situation itself may be complex, the response is not. There are five basic steps that need to be taken, with some variation in how they are implemented: (a) Identify the person who appears at risk; (b) assess the environment to ensure that intervention is safe for you and the individual; (c) engage the individual in a dialogue about observable indicators and subjective symptoms of distress; (d) assess for safety; and (e) coordinate a plan for treatment engagement. Each of these steps is discussed individually in line with Figure 4.1.

The first step in Figure 4.1 is identifying an individual who appears at risk. We have described a number of different symptoms, behaviors, and indicators characteristic of psychosis and early psychosis in adoles-cents and young adults. The "better safe than sorry" approach should be initiated as early as possible after the first symptoms or behaviors are

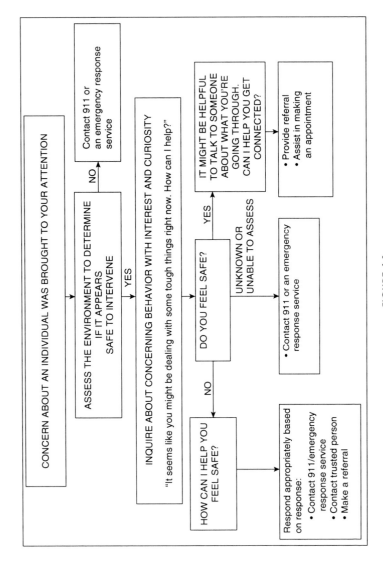

FIGURE 4.1
Decision tree.

identified. The identification may come from you as the primary observer, a colleague, a student, or an employer. Regardless of who observes the first signs, if you are being approached for help in addressing the concern we ask that you facilitate the steps toward treatment.

After a person at risk has been identified, the next step is to quickly evaluate the environment to determine whether an attempt at engagement is safe at the current time. For example, is the situation itself and the observable behavior of the individual such that you can initiate a conversation? Examples of unsafe environments include any aggression or threat on the part of the individual, or an unsafe setting where impulsive reactions could lead to harm (e.g., close to a busy street). Again, it will be hard to predict how a person is going to react to what may be perceived as an intrusive and difficult conversation. If you are unsure if the person is safe, then it is best to initiate an emergency intervention.

If it is determined that the environment is safe, the next step is engaging the individual in a manner that will allow for a conversation about his or her subjective experience and level of distress, as well as the concerns voiced by others, if appropriate. At this juncture, it is important to demonstrate empathy and interest, rather than confrontation or force. It is important to remember that the early period of psychosis is a very vulnerable time, fraught with fear, confusion, anger, anxiety, and the like. Although we have provided examples of many different symptom presentations, you will likely not know much about the specific symptoms a person is experiencing before you approach him or her. Yes, you may have some information from comments made to others, content of homework assignments, or observable behaviors, but that will only reflect a piece of the entire illness picture. Therefore, the initial engagement period is perhaps the most important step, as it will greatly inform the individual's level of collaboration with developing a plan to engage with treatment, and potentially his or her commitment to that plan. You may be the *first* person to ever have this type of conversation about these experiences, hence your critical role and the overall purpose of this book.

Step 4 in the decision tree is assessment of safety of the individual. Hopefully, rapport was established and a dialogue developed in step 2. If not, safety still needs to be assessed at some level. There are many methods of asking about safety and some are more direct than others. Regardless of what approach you choose, it is important to glean the following: (a) Does the person feel safe at this time? (b) Is there something that can be done to increase feelings of safety? (c) Are there thoughts about hurting himself or herself or someone else? The responses to these questions will also directly inform the level of treatment explored at that time; the level of immediate safety risk will dictate the route of treatment that should be pursued.

The final step is identifying some problematic behaviors or experiences and developing a plan for treatment engagement. Again, the route pursued will be dictated by the determination of safety. Reporting thoughts of suicide or self-harm or harm to someone else absolutely necessitates a call to 911. It is not your responsibility to substantiate intent or evaluate the likelihood of follow-through. This response is designed to protect and not to punish. Contacting 911 or another emergency number is also designated if the safety risk is unknown or unable to be assessed. Again, we encourage you to consider an approach of "better safe than sorry." The consequences of harm are much more detrimental than evaluation or admission to a psychiatric hospital.

If the individual has reported that he or she does not feel safe for one reason or another but is not endorsing any immediate safety concerns, there are a number of options at your disposal, and most of these have been described in the "Developing a Plan" section in this chapter. Lastly, if there do not appear to be any acute issues or risk or distress, then it is most appropriate to provide referral resources and connect with family or friends, if appropriate. It may be helpful to present intervention options and facilitate the person's connecting the most appropriate one. You may even assist in making an appointment with one of the resources in your area. Strategies for identifying resources can also be found in the "Developing a Plan" section in this chapter.

When initiating these steps in the decision tree, it is important to proceed through each step until the end, even if the previous step was not successfully negotiated. For example, if someone has been identified as "at risk" based on the symptoms and criteria we have outlined thus far but refuses to discuss how he or she is feeling or address the concerns of others, attempts should still be made to evaluate safety. If the reticence continues, then developing a treatment plan should then be addressed. This may mean that your only option is to call 911 or another emergency service because you cannot evaluate safety or identify alternative treatment routes. This is a perfect example of the "better safe than sorry" approach.

FINAL CONSIDERATIONS

We would like to close this chapter with a list of general "Dos and Don'ts" (Table 4.1). Many of these have been introduced and addressed at various points throughout the text. However, we would like you to have a quick reference to what we feel are the nuts and bolts of a successful interaction.

TABLE 4.1
Dos and Don'ts

Do	Example
Speak in a calm tone	Not too high or too low—demonstrate stability, calm
Ask questions that are simple and direct	One question at a time. Concise, jargon-free statements and questions
Be knowledgeable about your program's policy for reporting high-risk students	You should be aware of your organization's policies and procedures for reporting these events to ensure that the appropriate protocol is in place and the rights of everyone involved (including the adolescent or young adult) are protected
Identify reason for intervention/ concern	"I would like to talk to you about the paper you turned in for class. Some of what you wrote concerned me."
Inquire about the individual's understanding of the situation	"Do you understand why I stopped you in the hallway?"
Inquire about the individual's response to the situation	"Please tell me how you feel about what I've said/witnessed."
Ask about safety[a]	"Do you feel safe in this office?" "Is there a place where you would feel safer while we talk?"
Ask about thoughts and/or plans to harm self or others	"Are you having any thoughts about hurting yourself?" " Are you having any thoughts to harm anyone?"
Ask to call trusted friends or family	"Who can I call to be here with you while we discuss a plan?"
Attempt to collaborate on a plan	"I'd like to talk to you about getting some help/support for this issue." "What would be most helpful right now?" "How do you think we should proceed?"
Acknowledge and reflect participation	"Thank you for sharing and helping me understand the situation."

(continued)

TABLE 4.1 (*continued*)
Dos and Don'ts

Do	Example
Inform about some or all of the intervention plan (this may differ based on the individual's level of agitation)	"I think it may be helpful to meet with Mr. Cliff, the school psychologist. He is very knowledgeable about the areas we talked about today and I believe he can help you manage some of these difficulties. Let's leave him a message together."
Ask permission	"Would it be okay if I ask you a few questions about what happened yesterday?" "Do you mind if I sit next to you?"

ᵃSee this chapter for explicit instructions on how to do this if you are not a licensed mental health professional.

Don't	Example
Be afraid to intervene	If you are reading this book, then these situations will likely be "your business" at some point
Be afraid to ask questions	Asking a question does not give someone the "idea" to do something
Be afraid to share concern with colleagues	You will likely need support around this situation (e.g., emotional, administrative). Maintain privacy where confidentiality applies
Feel responsible for answering the "how," "what," and "why" of these situations	You do not need to answer these types of questions to be helpful or to facilitate engagement with appropriate treatment
Fully accept "I'm okay" or "I don't need help"	Despite all of your best efforts you may not get any response and/or your attempt to facilitate an intervention plan may be squashed. However, employ the "better safe than sorry" approach to connect with care

(continued)

TABLE 4.1 *(continued)*
Dos and Don'ts

Don't	Example
Fall victim to diffusion of responsibility/bystander effect	Do not assume that someone else will step in who witnessed the concerning events or is aware of the details and risk. He or she will be assuming the same about you!
Confront or challenge psychotic content	It is not your responsibility to "reason" with the individuals or alter their beliefs. Challenging their experiences will only bring about conflict and will thwart any attempt at intervention
Threaten intervention or introduce ultimatums	The goal of this guide is to facilitate connection with treatment. This is much more successful when there is some collaboration present. Collaboration is best achieved with the strategies introduced in Chapter 5. When this is not possible, the "better safe than sorry" approach is encouraged
Make promises you can't keep	"You won't be hospitalized." "You won't be asked to leave school."
Make physical contact without asking	Even contact that you might see as supportive, like a pat on the shoulder, could be perceived as dangerous by someone who is experiencing psychosis. Instead consider verbal methods of showing support with empathy

There are many details that you will not be aware of or be able to control in a given interaction—that is the expectation. Knowing that, these Dos and Don'ts will ensure a greater likelihood of an effective, successful interaction, even with all of the other "unknowns."

EXHIBIT 4.1: **ANDRE**

Andre's philosophy professor, Dr. Wall, was shocked when he read Andre's most recent writing assignment. Instead of responding to the assignment, Andre had written a nearly incoherent series of statements about his feelings of being targeted by peers. It was difficult for Dr. Wall to figure out exactly what Andre was trying to communicate, but it was clear that his thinking was not making sense and that he felt unable to trust his classmates. Dr. Wall decided that he would talk to Andre in person after class in order to try to better understand what was happening.

Andre did not get up at the end of class. Instead, he watched intently as each of his classmates packed up and exited the room. Dr. Wall approached him with the assignment in hand.

DR. WALL: Andre, I was hoping we could talk for a minute. Is it okay if I sit down?

ANDRE: That's fine.

DR. WALL: I am pretty concerned about what I read in your most recent assignment. It seems really different than your usual writing. Is there anything going on that you might want to talk about?

ANDRE: No. Why?

DR. WALL: Well, it really struck me how angry you're feeling with your classmates. Did something happen?

ANDRE: The usual stuff. They're liars and they want to make sure that I know I'm failing. That I'm not one of them. They always make sure everyone knows. Haven't you seen it?

DR. WALL: That sounds really upsetting. I haven't noticed, but I'm usually pretty busy with stuff up front, so I might miss things sometimes. Do you feel safe being in class with them?

ANDRE: I know I could defend myself. I'm on guard all the time. If they keep looking at me, I'll take care of them.

DR. WALL: It sounds like you're really scared. What do you mean "take care of them"?

ANDRE: Whatever I have to do. I'll hurt them if I need to. I don't want to, but I will.

DR. WALL: You must be really worried if you're considering that. I'm pretty worried too. I want to make sure you feel safe, and that you don't feel like you would need to hurt someone. Sometimes when people are feeling really scared it helps to talk to a doctor. Would you be willing to go to the emergency department and talk to someone about what you're going through?

ANDRE: I'm not crazy. I don't need a doctor. What I need is for everyone to leave me alone.

DR. WALL: All of this sounds really upsetting. Would you like me to walk over to the counseling center with you so you could talk to someone?

ANDRE: You're not getting it. There is only one thing to do.

Andre stormed out of the room. Dr. Wall took note of the direction he headed and what he was wearing as he dialed 911 to tell them what had transpired and that he was concerned about Andre's ability to stay safe. He described to them the assignment that Andre had turned in and the conversation they had. He also shared with them that Andre appears to be very fearful and might be easily scared and asked if they would be able to approach without sirens and with minimal people. Dr. Wall stayed on the phone and continued to watch Andre from the classroom window so that he could continue to describe to responders where he was and what he was doing.

Discussion. Andre does not appear receptive to the idea of connecting with a mental health professional at this point; however, because he also mentions the possibility of hurting someone, he leaves Dr. Wall with little choice about what must be done. As Dr. Wall is a professor and not a mental health provider, he needs to have Andre evaluated by a qualified professional to determine whether Andre is safe to be in the community and whether he might need a more intensive level of care. He attempted to assist Andre in getting to the counseling center to achieve this, but Andre was not interested.

Dr. Wall's experience is not uncommon. Even when the person trying to assist someone in psychiatric crisis is using the appropriate skills and has good intentions, the outcome might not always be as desired. The most important goal, though, is that the safety of all parties is protected, which Dr. Wall was able to do by involving emergency services appropriately.

EXHIBIT 4.2: **DEENA**

Deena showed up for her doctor's appointment looking disheveled and upset. It had been a year since her last checkup and the notes in her chart did not mention anything about being unkempt. It was obvious that she had been crying, but when the assistant at the front desk asked her what was wrong, she shook her head hard from side to side and went to sit in the waiting room. While she was waiting, Deena was seen mumbling to herself and making jerking movements as if swatting something out of her eyes.

When the nurse came to retrieve Deena from the waiting room, she had to call Deena's name three times before Deena stood up. Deena did not respond to the nurse's friendly greeting or inquiry about her day. Instead, she kept her eyes fixed on the floor without speaking more than "okay" or offering a nod to show that she understood. She followed the nurse's directions to step onto the scale and to roll up her sleeve to have her blood pressure taken, but it was clear to the nurse that Deena was not feeling well and it may not been a purely physical problem. The nurse was concerned, but noted that Deena appeared to be physically unharmed, did not appear to have a weapon, and was not in immediate danger while she was in the office. However, she was concerned about Deena leaving the office alone.

NURSE: Deena, I can't help but notice that you seem to be having a hard time looking at me today. Is everything okay?

DEENA: Fine.

NURSE: It seems like you may have been upset or afraid earlier. I can see that your eyes are a little red. I know that mine get like that when I've been upset. Have you been feeling upset or afraid?

DEENA: I don't know. Not really.

NURSE: Do you feel safe to leave the office when you're finished here?

DEENA: I don't know.

NURSE: Is there anything specific you are worried might happen?

DEENA: I don't know. Maybe.

NURSE: Are you feeling worried enough that you might want to go to the emergency department and talk to a doctor there? They do a great job of helping people feel safe. I could see if we could have someone ride over with you in the ambulance if you don't want to go alone. Would that be helpful?

DEENA: No hospitals. I don't know...

NURSE: Deena, I'm concerned that you might be feeling upset or afraid. I'd like to help. I think we still have your mother's phone number in your file. If it is okay with you I'd like to call her so that we can make sure you are feeling okay when you leave. Would it be okay with you if I did that?

DEENA: That's fine. I don't care.

NURSE: Thanks, Deena, that makes me feel better. I'll be back with a sheet that I will need you to sign saying that I can call your mother. Then we can figure out what we can do together to get you feeling a little better.

Discussion. Deena had a very difficult time offering the nurse information that would help the nurse determine whether Deena was safe or not. The nurse opted to use a more directive approach in developing a plan by proposing one and offering Deena the option to reject it, rather than encouraging Deena to be more active in the development of the plan. It seems likely that Deena would not have been able to do that at the present time.

The nurse took stock of the situational factors and determined that calling emergency services was not immediately necessary; however, she did offer Deena the option of going to the hospital and strived to find a way to make that experience less scary. Because Deena did not seem to be in immediate danger, the nurse did not continue to push the hospital as an option, but instead tried to find an alternative that was more comfortable for Deena. The nurse was able to have Deena agree that she could talk to her mother, which would allow the nurse to share her concerns and observations and make a suggestion that Deena see a psychiatric provider if she does not already have one.

EXHIBIT 4.3: **JOEL**

Katie was cutting through the park to get to class on time, when she noticed Joel, a coworker of hers at the convenience store just off campus. Katie did not know Joel well and always found him odd, and recently she had noticed him talking to himself at work and behaving in odd ways. Last week he refused to come out of the freezer case even though he was clearly cold. When he tried to explain why he would not come out, his explanation did not make any sense. A few days later, the manager sent Joel home because he suspected that he was drunk or on drugs. Katie had assumed he was probably right. But when she saw him curled in a ball sitting under a tree talking to someone she could not see, she wanted to make sure he was okay. He was speaking loudly and she could hear him clearly from several feet away. She slowly approached him and announced her presence.

KATIE: Joel? It's Katie, from work.

Joel did not look up or respond, but continued talking in a manner she could not understand.

KATIE: How are you?

Joel shrugged.

KATIE: Are you talking to someone?

Joel flinched, and looked up at her, but did not respond.

KATIE: I have to get to class in a few minutes, but would it be okay if I sit down with you for a second before I go?

Joel nodded and moved over slightly. Katie waited a minute or two before speaking again, allowing Joel to adjust to being in her company. Joel continued his internal conversation, but quieted his volume slightly.

KATIE: Is everything okay? It seems like you might be a little worried about something.

JOEL: Why?

KATIE: Why would I ask that? Well, you're huddled up over here all alone. Sometimes when I'm worried I want to huddle up alone too. Are you feeling worried?

Joel nodded slightly.

KATIE: Do you feel safe?

JOEL: I'm fine. I'll be fine.

KATIE: Do you want to tell me what you're worried about?

Joel shook his head "no."

KATIE: Okay, well if you change your mind, let me know. Is there anyone you would like to talk to about it? Anyone I could call for you to talk to?

JOEL: My doctor knows.

KATIE: Your doctor, great. Do you happen to have your doctor's number? I could help you call if you want me to.

Joel nodded and rooted around in his wallet for a moment before handing Katie a crumpled appointment card with the doctor's phone number on it.

KATIE: Would you like me to talk?

Joel didn't respond and continued muttering to himself.

KATIE: I'm going to call and you let me know if you want to talk instead, okay?

No response.

Katie dialed the phone and connected to the receptionist.

KATIE: Hi, I'm here with Joel who I believe is a patient of Dr. Ramirez. He's having a pretty rough time and mentioned that he's been worried about some things. I'm pretty worried about him. He asked me to call Dr. Ramirez for him in case he could help.

The receptionist informed Katie that she could not confirm whether Joel was a patient of Dr. Ramirez's due to confidentiality.

KATIE: Okay, Joel, they can't talk to me, but they can talk to you. If you want to put it on speaker I can help, but they need to hear you.

JOEL: Hi. I need to see Dr. Ramirez.

The receptionist informed Joel that he had missed his last appointment and his next was not until next week. She said she would pass the message along to Dr. Ramirez, but that she did not think he could be seen sooner. She added, if he felt that it was an emergency he could go to the ER.

KATIE: Do you think you need to go to the ER? I could walk with you if you want.
JOEL: No. I'm fine. I just need to see Dr. Ramirez.
KATIE: Okay, do you think you'll be okay until next week?

Joel nodded.

KATIE: I'm glad. But would it be okay if I get your phone number and I give you mine, just in case. I'd love to talk to you tomorrow and make sure you're still feeling okay. You seem pretty worried.
JOEL: Okay.

Discussion. In this example, we see how difficult it can be to gather information from someone who is experiencing psychosis. In many instances, Joel was not able to verbally respond to Katie. However, Katie was able to use simplified questions that allowed Joel to communicate with brief responses or nonverbal signals. Katie was able to connect Joel with a current provider, but ran into a barrier that many well-intended helpers will face: confidentiality. Although confidentiality standards exist to protect patients receiving services, it can be frustrating for supportive others to run up against this obstacle. Thankfully, Katie was able to navigate around this by having Joel do some of the talking on the phone.

Unfortunately, Katie and Joel were not able to get immediate assistance for Joel by contacting Dr. Ramirez. Although this may be frustrating, it is a common experience in mental health. Even clients already connected to services may not be able to be seen quickly, and instead may be referred to ERs. This is not a fault of the provider, but rather a factor of how overwhelmed and understaffed mental health care services are. Because Joel did not want to go to the ER and was not able to see Dr. Ramirez right away, Katie opted to perform some follow-up actions. Given her casual but familiar relationship with Joel, this seems appropriate. It also provides Joel with an additional support, should he feel overwhelmed. Having this experience with Katie may mean he is more comfortable reaching out to her in the coming days if he should feel that he needs help.

EXHIBIT 4.4: **JAMIE**

Jamie was admitted to college with an academic scholarship to study pre-medicine; he had always been a dedicated student who preferred a quiet library to a wild party. His first semester on campus was tougher than he expected. Good grades came much easier in high school, and making new friends is a challenge when you are a little shy. Nonetheless, Jamie persevered through his first semester making A's and B's, and managed to develop good relationships with his roommates.

After returning from winter break for his second semester, Jamie's roommates noticed that he seemed to be acting differently. He seemed less interested in studying; he approached strangers and spoke to them without hesitation; he wanted to go out drinking more often and experimented with drugs. It was not that unusual at first, it just seemed like he had come out of his shell. Jamie's roommates liked this new, more outgoing Jamie! But as time went on, Jamie's behavior changed more dramatically and began to strain his relationship with his roommates. Jamie came in and out of the room at all hours of the night, with little regard for his sleeping roommates, and began filling his room with broken computer parts, old telephones, radios, and wires that did not seem to belong to anything. When his roommates asked him why he was keeping all this "junk," he responded with an explanation they could hardly follow; something about "building a scanner" that was going to "scan through the skull and show how music works in the brain." Jamie's roommates were growing tired of his odd behavior. They avoided him as much as possible, and one of them even moved out.

Jamie's teachers noticed a change too. Jamie rarely made it to class, and when he did he was late and made an entrance that drew the attention of the entire room. When he participated in class his responses did not make sense but he would not stop speaking long enough for anyone else to talk. Jamie was even asked to leave class on a couple of occasions for being disruptive. His grades suffered, and with midterms approaching his professors became concerned. Jamie's anatomy professor even pulled him aside after class one day to ask if everything was okay. Jamie told him he felt "great" and said that he was "exploring all the things that one should explore, all the worlds and all the places you can go." His

128

professor was confused, but was reassured that at least Jamie said he was feeling okay.

A few days later, campus police received a call from an employee in the cafeteria reporting a disturbance. They arrived to find Jamie wearing his pajamas shouting at a cafeteria employee. His words were hard to follow, but bystanders were able to gather that he was upset about something related to his "authority being undermined" and that he felt he was "a target for people to violate in any way possible."

The two campus officers responding to the call split up, one dispersed the crowd of bystanders that had accumulated while the other carefully approached Jamie from the side.

OFFICER MICHAELS: Hi there, I'm Officer Michaels. It seems like you're pretty upset. I thought I might be able to help. Would it be okay if I talk to you for a few minutes?

JAMIE: I don't have anything to say to you. I'm trying to get him to understand that I won't be manipulated or controlled. [trails off in unintelligible speech]

OFFICER MICHAELS: I don't blame you for not wanting to be manipulated, I wouldn't like that either.

Officer Michaels subtly waved the cafeteria employee away.

JAMIE: No. You wouldn't. But it is my daily life. I don't have time for this, I don't care about this. None of it.

Jamie appeared to be growing more agitated, so Officer Michaels responded with a calm demeanor.

OFFICER MICHAELS: It sounds like you have a lot going on right now. Would it be okay if we find someplace less public to talk about it?

Jamie didn't respond verbally, but walked with Officer Michaels out of the cafeteria to sit on a bench outside. Jamie spent the next few minutes speaking in ways that made little sense, fidgeting and talking about how he didn't have to talk to Officer Michaels.

JAMIE: I don't have to talk to you, you know. Not if I don't want to.

OFFICER MICHAELS: I know you don't have to, but I really appreciate that you are.

Officer Michaels let Jamie go on for a few minutes, and he seemed to calm down slightly.

OFFICER MICHAELS: Jamie, you've got an awful lot on your mind right now. Sometimes when people have a lot on their mind it is helpful to talk to someone about it. We have a counseling center right here on campus, I can show you where it is if you would like me to walk with you.

Jamie quickly shook his head.

JAMIE: I'm not going there, I feel fine, I just don't know what everyone's problem is.
OFFICER MICHAELS: Jamie, it sounds like some of the things that are going on right now are pretty scary. Do you feel like you're safe?
JAMIE: I'm going to make sure I'm safe. I have to take care of myself. I'll do what I have to do.
OFFICER MICHAELS: You know, the people who work at the counseling center, part of their job is to help people feel safe when there is scary stuff going on around them. I really think they might be able to help.
JAMIE: Fine. I'll go over there, but I'm not going to promise I'll talk to them. If I don't like them, I'm not talking.
OFFICER MICHAELS: That sounds like a plan to me.

Discussion. In this example, you can see that Jamie has experienced a marked change in his personality and behavior. The dramatic changes across areas of his life indicate a cause for worry, while the specifics of his odd behavior and incoherent language raise concern about the presence of psychosis. In addition to psychosis, Jamie's behavior appears to indicate a manic episode. It is common for individuals experiencing mania to report feeling good, or even better than usual, as Jamie did to his professor. It is also not uncommon for some people in a person's life to enjoy aspects of their changing behavior, as Jamie's roommates did at first.

At the time when Officer Michaels intervened, Jamie appeared acutely agitated and upset. Officer Michaels chose not to respond with matching agitation or aggression, but rather took a calm stance that deescalated Jamie over time. He took measures to remove Jamie from a public situation with lots of people around. Situations with a lot of people, or with a lot of stimulation, can be overwhelming to someone with psychosis, so removing Jamie from this setting may have helped to engage him in a more productive line of conversation.

Officer Michaels reflected an understanding of what Jamie was saying, to show that he was listening, allowing him to develop a relationship with Jamie even in a brief period of time. Officer Michaels clearly felt that Jamie was experiencing a mental health issue, and immediately tried to take steps to bring him in contact with a mental health provider who could more thoroughly assess his condition and safety. However, Jamie was uninterested in speaking with someone at first, which is very common. Officer Michaels did not leave the discussion there, but rather tried to figure out how he could make such a contact feel helpful given Jamie's current perspective. He was able to ask about safety, and when Jamie did not appear to feel totally safe, he used this as an entry point to once again suggest talking to a professional. Luckily, in this instance, Jamie was agreeable to seeing someone. It is particularly helpful that Officer Michaels offered to walk him over. This way, he can be assured that Jamie arrives there safely and he is able to provide the staff at the counseling center with information regarding the incident that has occurred.

EXHIBIT 4.5: **KENYA**

Kenya had played for the field hockey team since she was a freshman. She never loved academics, but worked hard to keep her grades up so that she could play on the team. She was very close with her teammates, who became her best friends early on in high school. She loved going to the mall on weekends or to the community pool in the summer. She knew most of her teammates' parents and they knew hers because they frequented each other's houses so much. She also had a great relationship with her coach, Coach Harlan, who insisted that Kenya keep her grades up and even arranged for her to receive tutoring in chemistry when she was having trouble. The team was such an important part of her life. That is why it struck everyone as so strange when Kenya started to seem less invested during her senior year. At first, everyone thought it was "senioritis"—that Kenya was simply anxious to wrap up high school and head off to college. However, after she missed several weeks of practice and failed to show up to a teammate's birthday party, people began to worry. Instead of coming to practice, Kenya would dart out the back door of the school after the final bell rang. The whole team was talking about how much Kenya had changed. She did not seem to want to hang out at all anymore. When her friends asked about the changes, she said she had to "study." She canceled plans with friends because she wanted to go to church, even though no one had ever known Kenya to attend church other than on holidays. At one point, she told a teammate that she was studying the Qur'an, and at the same meeting mentioned that she planned to attend an evening mass at her family's Presbyterian church. When her friend asked about her sudden interest in so many different faiths, she responded that she is "all religions." Everyone was worried, but hoped that perhaps Kenya was just finding her faith and exploring belief systems like many young people do.

After not seeing Kenya for several weeks, Coach Harlan noticed her standing outside of the school watching while the field hockey team practiced. Coach Harlan called out to her, asking if she wanted to practice, but Kenya did not respond. Coach Harlan instructed the team to run some drills and walked over to Kenya.

COACH HARLAN: Kenya, we've really missed you! Is everything okay? We'd love for you to come join us.
KENYA: No. I can't today.

Kenya stared at the ground and didn't look up at Coach Harlan.

COACH HARLAN: Okay, well maybe another day then.

Coach Harlan started to walk away. She didn't want to push Kenya or make her feel forced.

KENYA: No. I won't be here anymore.
COACH HARLAN: What do you mean you won't be here? Where will you be?
KENYA: I'll be dead by then. Soon. It's all going to happen faster than I can play.

Kenya's voice was flat, and matter-of-fact, taking Coach Harlan off guard because she was discussing such an upsetting topic.

COACH HARLAN: What do you mean, Kenya? Why would you be dead? I don't want anything to happen to you.
KENYA: It has to happen. It's all written down. It's everywhere. I have to be gone to make it work.
COACH HARLAN: I'm not sure what you mean, Kenya, but if you want to come talk in my office for a minute I'd like that.
KENYA: No.
COACH HARLAN: Okay, maybe we could sit in the courtyard?
KENYA: No. I don't have time.
COACH HARLAN: Okay, I understand that. But, I do really miss talking to you, and what you just said worries me. Is there anything I can do to help?
KENYA: No.
COACH HARLAN: Would you like me to call your mom? Sometimes talking to someone you trust is helpful.
KENYA: No, that's okay. I just want to sit down for a minute.
COACH HARLAN: Okay. That's a great idea. Can I come back and check on you in a minute?
KENYA: That's fine.

Coach Harlan headed inside the school to find help. She approached another coach and asked him to talk with Kenya for a few minutes while she made some calls to make sure she was safe. He agreed, and went outside to talk with her.

Coach Harlan contacted her supervisor, and relayed her interaction with Kenya. She expressed concern for Kenya's safety and described her odd statements about being dead. Her supervisor recommended that she first call Kenya's mom, as she was not yet 18 years of age, and share her concerns, then call emergency services to have Kenya evaluated. Coach Harlan reached out to Kenya's mother and shared her concerns. She indicated that she was concerned enough that she felt Kenya may need to be evaluated by a doctor. With understandable reluctance, her mother agreed and indicated that she would come to the school to meet Kenya and go to the hospital with her. Coach Harlan then called 911 and explained the situation. She described what Kenya was saying and the recent changes in her behavior, as well as what she was wearing and her physical appearance. She asked that they not use lights or sirens if possible, and said she would be waiting with Kenya when they arrived. She then went back outside to sit with Kenya until the ambulance arrived.

Discussion. In this example, Kenya appears to have demonstrated a notable change in her behavior over time. In addition to isolating herself socially, not engaging in previously enjoyed activities, and challenges in communicating coherently, Kenya also appears to have developed a delusional system that is somehow related to religious material. Although it is natural for many young people to explore various faiths, the apparent connection between her exploration of new faiths and her statements of impending death makes this undoubtedly concerning.

Coach Harlan had to respond quickly to some worrisome comments from Kenya. Although they were vague and unclear comments, Coach Harlan responded appropriately by connecting Kenya to professionals when she was concerned. It is still possible that Kenya could refuse to go with the ambulance drivers, and unless they feel that she is a potential harm to herself or others, she cannot be forced to go. However, this is a determination that the emergency responders must make. Coach Harlan was in a very difficult position of having to make a decision about calling 911. Luckily, she was able to receive the support of a supervisor who could guide her through the process and make recommendations for specific actions.

EXHIBIT 4.6: **AIDEN**

Aiden was a shy, sweet, well-mannered kid, until his junior year of high school. He had always mostly kept to himself, performed adequately at school, and preferred video games and comic books to partying. He had a few close friends that he had grown up with, but mostly seemed to prefer solitary activities. During his junior year this changed. Aiden fell in with a crowd that loved the same comic books and video games he did, but also smoked marijuana and used alcohol frequently. At first, Aiden's parents were concerned, but not panicked; after all it is relatively normal for young people to experiment with substances. They tightened the rules on Aiden, requiring that he get a job at the local convenience store to keep him busy after school, and keeping a closer eye on his activities on the weekends. Despite their efforts, Aiden still seemed to manage to find his way into trouble. He was smoking marijuana more frequently, he seemed "out of it" when his parents tried to talk to him, and although his grades were never outstanding they dropped dramatically. Before long Aiden found himself in more serious trouble after a series of shoplifting charges landed him on juvenile probation.

Shortly after his probation began, Aiden started isolating himself. He refused to talk to his parents unless absolutely necessary, and even went out with his friends less frequently. He became a very picky eater, which was new to his parents. He refused to eat anything his father cooked, and insisted that only his mother could touch his food. He still smoked marijuana, despite the potential for this to get him in trouble with probation, but more often smoked alone than with his friends as he used to.

Aiden's probation officer, Catherine, saw him every few weeks to check in and make sure he was doing okay. She had taken a particular liking to him because he seemed like a good kid who was struggling. Over the course of a few meetings, Catherine noticed that Aiden was behaving more strangely. He was having trouble staying on the topic of their conversations, and often veered off into subjects that did not seem related at all. At their most recent meeting, after they had finished their usual check-in business, Aiden took off on a tangent. She could barely follow what he was saying, and when she asked him to explain, he grew irritated with her. He started talking about a group of kids from school who were hacking into his computer and reading his e-mail, taking mail out of the family's mailbox, and threatening to poison the family dog. At first, she thought he might be high, but she noted that he did not smell like marijuana, and his eyes were not bloodshot. Besides, she did not think he was acting like someone under the influence of marijuana. This was much different. Obviously concerned, Catherine tried to understand what was happening. She decided to approach Aiden to share her thoughts.

CATHERINE: I'm having trouble following you, Aiden, but it sounds like you're pretty concerned about these kids at school bothering you and threatening your dog.

AIDEN: Not bothering me. Trying to hurt everyone. Starting with the mail. The mailman doesn't know, it's hard to explain.

CATHERINE: Things are pretty scary right now. What can I do to help you feel safer?

AIDEN: I need them to stop. I just want peace.

CATHERINE: I can understand that. Is there someone I can call who might be able to help? Your parents?

AIDEN: No. I don't trust them. Them and the mailman. It's not for them to understand.

CATHERINE: Okay. This sounds very complicated, and I'm having a little trouble following it. I'd really like to help, Aiden. This seems really scary. Sometimes it helps to talk to a professional when scary things like this are going on. Would you like me to help you meet with someone who knows about this kind of thing?

AIDEN: I don't think anyone knows.

CATHERINE: I'm willing to bet someone does. I know it might not seem like talking will help, but sometimes meeting with a doctor or therapist to talk about scary things can help. Do you think you'd be willing to give that a try?

AIDEN: I don't think it will help. I don't need a doctor. I need them to leave me alone. I have to go.

CATHERINE: Okay, but can I ask if you feel safe enough to leave? You seem pretty worried.

AIDEN: I'll be fine, I just can't go near the mailbox, and I need to keep my dog inside. It will be okay if I stay home.

CATHERINE: Are you sure I can't help you connect with someone to talk to?

AIDEN: No. I don't feel like talking anymore.

CATHERINE: Okay. We have done a lot of talking today. Would it be okay if I give you a call tomorrow?

AIDEN: I don't know why, but okay.

CATHERINE: Thanks, Aiden. Please call me if you need anything. I will see you in a few weeks.

Aiden left, and Catherine called her supervisor to discuss the interaction. Her supervisor asked her to call Aiden's parents, since he was not yet 18 years old, and discuss with them what happened. She shared her experience with them and conveyed her concern for Aiden's well-being. She also offered them contact information for several mental health service centers in the area, including one she heard of that specializes in evaluating for psychosis, where Aiden may be able to obtain treatment.

Discussion. In this scenario, Catherine was having a difficult time understanding what Aiden was trying to communicate to her. Instead of becoming bogged down in understanding the details of his concerns, she focused on conveying her understanding of his feelings. Clearly, he was scared and upset by what was happening. Catherine focused on responding to these feelings. She was able to get some information from Aiden about whether he felt safe, and offered to connect him with services. As frequently happens, Aiden declined those services. However, with her supervisor's guidance, Catherine was able to take the extra step of passing along information to Aiden's parents who have a better likelihood of encouraging him to obtain treatment. At this point, Catherine has done all she can. Although it may be frustrating for her to not have been able to connect Aiden directly with services, she has taken an important step in communicating her concerns to his parents, and suggesting resources for assistance.

EXHIBIT 4.7: **COPING PLAN**

I will distract myself and keep myself busy with things that I like to do. These activities include:

_____

_____

_____

_____

I may get nervous before my first appointment with the therapist or counselor. I can stay positive by reminding myself of the benefits of treatments. Some helpful thoughts may be:

_____

_____

_____

_____

During this process, it will be helpful to talk to other people who care about me and whom I trust about my concerns, about treatment, and about anything else I am going through.

Name: Phone Number:

_____

_____

_____

_____

CHAPTER **FIVE**

Follow-Up and Outcomes

This section of the chapter provides many optional approaches to consider after the initial intervention has occurred. For professionals who are likely to encounter the individual after the period of crisis because of a previous relationship or the particular environment, guidance is provided regarding strategies for developing a plan for "next steps." These steps may range from identifying mental health resources, organizing accommodations, or identifying potential advocates. When appropriate, facilitating additional involvement from families or caregivers is also discussed where appropriate. Many of these are presented in list form and are applicable to individuals with various levels of skill and training and in a variety of domains. The notion of appropriateness is clearly explicated to discourage inappropriate follow-up, protect confidentiality, and decrease additional intervention outside of areas of competence.

In some ways, the act of assisting a young adult with psychosis is an *event*. The interaction may be relatively brief, or not, but eventually, the actual interaction in which you attempt to assist the individual is over. In other ways, however, it is less of an event and more of a *process*. That is, the discrete beginning and end of your involvement are sometimes not clearly defined. In this chapter, we discuss a variety of potential outcomes of intervention and treatment dispositions, as well as suggestions to guide follow-up contact with the young person and recommendations for self-care following your contact with the young adult experiencing psychosis.

POTENTIAL OUTCOMES FOLLOWING YOUR INTERVENTION

There are a number of potential outcomes that can occur from helping a young adult with psychosis. The individual may choose to participate in outpatient treatment. If the individual is deemed to be a potential danger to himself or herself or others, he or she may require hospitalization to stabilize symptoms. Alternatively, there is certainly a possibility that the individual will be disinterested in treatment and continue as he or she was prior to your efforts to intervene. The potential outcomes are varied and depend on a number of important factors including the severity of symptoms, potential for dangerousness, insight into symptoms, and motivation for change.

Declining All Treatment Options

It is important to consider that at a certain point the individual's well-being is out of your hands. This may be because you have connected the individual with an appropriate professional who has now taken the lead, or because the person is simply not interested in the assistance you have to offer. Let us consider an example:

> Ray's biology professor has been concerned about him after observing him in a heated exchange with another student. The professor attempts to calm Ray, but is unable to do so and notes that Ray is not making sense when he speaks. The professor calls for emergency services to evaluate Ray, but they determine that Ray is not a danger to himself or others, and therefore does not qualify for involuntary hospitalization. The responders offer to connect him with outpatient services at the college, and encourage him to seek treatment. Ray expresses that he does not think there is anything wrong, and that he is not interested in treatment. Frustrated and feeling strongly that Ray is in need of help, the professor continues to encourage Ray to reach out to a treatment provider, but Ray declines.

Of course, we hope that young adults experiencing psychosis will be agreeable to professional intervention and seeking treatment and go on to achieve success in recovery. However, this is not always the case. It is not uncommon for a young adult with psychosis to flatly refuse to engage in treatment. This may be due to a number of different factors, many of which were discussed in the "Typical Responses" section of Chapter 3. Despite our good intentions, attempts to convince the young person are often futile. If the young adult in question is older than 18 years, we must respect his or her autonomy and the right to make this decision, the exception being situations in which the young person may be in danger or may endanger others, or under guardianship. If the young adult is younger than 18 years, you may have options to involve parents or a guardian in order to facilitate treatment. Even so, each individual's pathway to treatment is unique and it is important to respect the fact that not all individuals may be "ready" for treatment. This does not mean that your efforts have been in vain, or that your options for helping are depleted.

Even in cases in which the individual has not been able to engage in treatment, it is important to acknowledge the value of a positive, supportive, and accepting interaction, and the potential future benefit of such interactions. For instance, the individual may not be ready to engage in treatment at the given time, but if he or she had a positive experience with a supportive person, the individual may seek out that person should he or she feel the need for additional support or guidance, if or when he or she does decide to look into the treatment options.

Hospitalization

As we mentioned earlier, in cases where an individual is evaluated by a medical or mental health professional and determined to be a danger to himself or herself or others, the individual may require hospitalization in order to ensure safety and allow for the opportunity to reduce symptoms. Individuals may be admitted to a psychiatric facility *voluntarily*, meaning he or she has agreed to take part in inpatient treatment. Or the individual may be remanded to treatment *involuntarily* if he or she is determined to be a danger to himself or herself or others by a medical or mental health professional but refuses to take part in voluntary inpatient treatment. Each state has its own laws and regulations for how such admissions may occur and who is qualified to conduct the evaluations that could result in such a hospitalization. If you have concerns about safety, seek assistance from emergency services or a mental health professional who will be able to provide you with information about how this process works in your state. However, this decision will not be your responsibility.

During an acute hospitalization, there are a number of steps taken in order to provide the individual with the best care possible. First, a team of medical and mental health professionals complete a variety of assessments, both physical and psychological, in order to determine the specific nature of the problem. The controlled environment of the hospital allows the providers to treat the problems more aggressively than they would in outpatient treatment settings because they are able to carefully monitor the young person's response to medications and other interventions. Often, psychiatric medications require a trial of several days to several weeks to ensure that the individual will benefit from a medication and that any side effects will be tolerable. Inpatient care also typically consists of groups or classes designed to provide information about mental illness and assist individuals in managing symptoms. In addition to educational groups, there are often a variety of activities offered to provide a schedule and structure to the day. There is also time for individuals to have visits from family or friends, use the phone, and in some cases communicate via e-mail or Facebook.

Although time in the hospital can be valuable and extremely helpful in beginning to reduce an individual's psychiatric symptoms, it is also not an optimal environment for recovery. It distances many of the individual's social supports, and is likely to keep the individual from engaging in productive activities such as school or work. For these reasons, determining an appropriate and effective discharge plan is a focus of the inpatient team from the time the person arrives. Such a plan often involves identifying supportive people in the young adult's life, determining where appropriate treatment can be provided when the individual leaves the hospital, and meeting other basic needs the individual may have such as housing or access to food. The goal of a psychiatric hospitalization is to provide a lot of intensive treatment in a controlled environment, over as short a time as possible. A successful hospitalization can help reduce active psychotic symptoms, increase an individual's ability to stay safe, and set the young adult up for a promising recovery.

However, for many individuals, even a successful psychiatric hospitalization is a scary, embarrassing, and upsetting experience, particularly if they did not voluntarily participate in the admission. Consider for a moment the symptoms described in Chapter 2 and how they might manifest in a situation in a hospital setting.

> Meg is petrified with fear, curled up under the covers of her bed refusing to come out. The doctors and nurses try to reassure her that they are there to help, but she is sure that they are trying to infect her with a deadly virus that will melt her insides. She cries and shouts when they enter the room, afraid that they have come to administer the virus.

They are always asking her to take pills. She has seen the
other patients walking around without concern, and is sure
that this is a sign they have already been infected. She's not
even sure who to trust anymore, since her own sister was
the one who initially brought her to the hospital and handed
her over to these people. She doesn't have anyone to talk to
about her concerns because she fears they will kill her if they
find out she is aware of the plot.

The hospital environment, although designed to treat, also puts
individuals in a new and potentially scary situation where they are sur-
rounded by people they do not know who are asking them to do things
based on authority and trust (something they likely have very little of at
the time, especially if they are experiencing paranoia). In addition, symptoms are likely to interact with the unfamiliarity of the situation, resulting
in delusional or hallucinatory content that is related to it. Also, you will
recall that stress can exacerbate psychotic and mood symptoms, and such
a situation would undoubtedly be stressful. However, this may be a necessary step toward recovery.

Outpatient Treatment

In an ideal situation, a person is able to stay safe and access treatment
services without a hospitalization. In this instance, there are a variety of
outpatient treatment options that might meet his or her needs. Outpatient
services refer to treatment programs where an individual does not reside
in the treatment facility. Outpatient services can differ in their intensity
and time requirements. For example, an intensive outpatient program or
a partial hospital program may consist of several days a week, and several hours a day of treatment. An individual might attend such a program
Monday through Friday from 9 a.m. until 2 p.m. Often such treatment
consists of group and individual therapies as well as medication management. Another possible outpatient treatment option is a more traditional
outpatient clinic. In this setting, an individual might see an individual
therapist weekly or biweekly for an hour and meet with a psychiatrist
monthly for anywhere from 15 minutes to an hour. This is clearly a less
intense treatment and allows the individual more time to engage in activities such as school or work as his or her symptoms reduce and functioning
improves. Outpatient treatment programs vary greatly in their structure
and intensity, as they are designed to meet the needs of individuals in
different stages of recovery.

TABLE 5.1
Summary of Potential Outcomes

Declining treatment	• Despite your best efforts, some individuals may not be prepared to engage in treatment • If the individual is not a danger to self or others and is older than 18 years, he or she cannot be involuntarily admitted to treatment

Hospitalization	• Strives to achieve two goals as quickly as possible
	  o Determine the nature of the problem and develop a treatment strategy
	  o Reduce symptom severity so that the individual can resume functioning outside of the hospital
	• May be voluntary or involuntary
	  o Voluntary—the individual agrees to take part in inpatient treatment
	  o Involuntary—the individual is deemed to be a danger to himself or herself or others by a medical or mental health professional and is remanded to an inpatient treatment facility
	• Medication trials likely to occur
	• Therapeutic and leisure activities to provide daily structure
	• Typically able to receive visits and phone calls from family and friends

Outpatient treatment	• Goals
	  o Provide therapeutic supports and treatment within the community
	  o Reduce symptoms so that they do not interfere with the life goals of the individual
	  o Reduce likelihood of future hospitalizations
	• Many possible settings with varying intensity of treatment
	  o More intensive treatments may consist of several hours per day of treatment, several days per week
	  o Less intensive treatments may consist of weekly or biweekly psychotherapy and monthly medication management

In recent years, an additional resource has become available in many places in the form of specialized treatment programs for young adults experiencing the early stages of psychotic illness. These programs also tend to vary greatly in the structure of their services; however, they are similar in that they specialize in working with young adults to prevent a chronic course of psychotic illness and improve chances of recovery. An added benefit of these programs is an opportunity to meet other adolescents or young adults with similar difficulties. This helps to normalize the experience while also building skills within a peer group setting. You will also recall that social isolation is a common symptom that accompanies psychosis; so having an opportunity to connect with peers can be a helpful intervention in and of itself. Table 5.1 provides a summary of the possible outcome dispositions discussed.

WHAT IS THE BEST WAY FOR YOU TO FOLLOW-UP?

Following the acute period of intervention, it may be appropriate to offer continued support to a young adult with psychosis whom you may have assisted getting connected with treatment, particularly if you still have concerns about the young person's mental health or well-being. In this section, we discuss a variety of considerations related to the appropriateness of follow-up as well as suggestions for maximizing the benefit of follow-up contacts.

The appropriateness of follow-up and continued involvement with a young adult with psychosis will vary greatly depending on your profession and the nature of your relationship with the individual. For instance, if you are a high school guidance counselor who has had a long-standing relationship with the young adult, it is likely that you will find it to be appropriate to follow up and offer continued support. However, if you are a college campus police officer who encountered the young adult in response to a call, it is less likely to be appropriate to follow up. In general, we would like to offer the following points for consideration as to whether follow-up is appropriate.

Obligations and Limitations of Professions

Many professions have standards of conduct and ethical obligations that govern behavior. We encourage you to consider your professional obligations and how they may apply to such a situation. If you are unsure of these obligations and limitations, discuss them with a supervisor prior to providing any follow-up support. Some professions may be required to follow-up in particular ways, for instance, documenting the incident, reporting the incident to a superior, or following up with the young adult in a particular way. If you are a mental health professional, you may have obligations related to your licensure.

Experience and Training

When we witness someone in crisis, it is an understandable urge to want to solve the problem, to offer advice, and to have opinions regarding how a situation should be handled based on our personal life experience. Although these are well-intended and often seemingly harmless efforts, they may not involve the best use of the resources each individual "helper" can offer. Every individual will bring to the situation a unique set of skills that can be helpful and we encourage those assisting in such a situation to be aware of their strengths as well as their limitations as a helping party. For example, following an initial contact with a young adult experiencing psychosis, a teacher may have the ability to liaison with school administration to ensure that they are aware of the challenges the individual is experiencing, or to ensure that the individual receives accommodations from which he or she might benefit. A residence life coordinator at a college might be able to assist the individual in advocating for single-room housing or offer social support by encouraging the individual to take part in activities. A sibling or friend might be able to offer support in helping an individual remember to take his or her medication daily. And, of course, any one of these people could show concern and care with a simple "How are you doing?"

In order to provide the best support for an individual in psychiatric crisis, it is important that those assisting are aware of the scope of their training. Many individuals who are able to assist in an acute psychiatric crisis are not trained to provide psychotherapeutic treatment, diagnostic assessment, or other more formal interventions. However, they may be able to offer valuable emotional support and assistance in accessing services. The most helpful resources to the individual are going to be those that you are most able to provide. When considering plans for follow-up contact, reflect on your unique strengths and the resources at your disposal that could help meet the individual's needs.

Requests of the Individual

Sometimes an individual will state a clear preference whether or not he or she is open to follow-up contacts and continued support. For instance, he or she may stipulate "You can ask me how I'm doing, but I don't want you to ask me if I'm taking my medication" *or* "I would like your help making an appointment with a counselor, but I want to go by myself." Moreover, the individual may indicate that he or she is not open to additional supports at the present time. Provided that safety is not a concern, it is best to respect the individual's wishes, within the confines of any professional boundaries, of course. If safety *is* a concern, we encourage you to use the "better safe than sorry" approach and involve a medical or mental health professional immediately by using emergency services such as 911 or a local emergency department.

If an individual has not explicitly stated a preference for continued contact, consider the risks and benefits, *for the adolescent or young adult,* of initiating a follow-up contact. Experiencing a psychotic episode can be very confusing, scary, or embarrassing, and encountering individuals who were involved in the intervention can bring about a number of different reactions for the adolescent or young adult. If you do decide to initiate follow-up contact, be considerate of the circumstances surrounding the contact (e.g., setting) and what you would like to communicate. For instance, it is likely to be more appropriate to discuss such a sensitive topic in a relatively private park as opposed to a crowded cafeteria where the person is sitting with his or her friends. Also, consider the goals of your follow-up. Take stock of your motivations and consider whether those goals can be realistically met and if they are in the best interest of the young adult. For instance, if you feel a desire to follow-up in order to demonstrate your knowledge of working with young adults with psychosis, or if you hope to offer advice to the person about how to fix his or her problems, it may be best to refrain from following up. Although these are understandable and natural responses, they may not be as helpful to the young adult and may actually cause unintentional harm. It is important that all follow-up is done with the best interest of the young person in mind. It is not your responsibility or obligation to follow-up after the initial interaction unless your profession is such that you are engaged in the treatment or aftercare plan. Thus, carefully consider the contact you may initiate.

Personal Comfort Level

Ideally, the process of assisting a young adult experiencing psychosis is a positive experience for both parties involved, meaning that the young adult feels supported, heard, and helped, and the "helper" feels safe, effective, and confident in his or her ability to assist. Along these lines, attending to your own comfort level regarding follow-up contacts is important.

If you feel wary or uncomfortable with additional contact with the individual, it is likely to be most helpful to both parties to keep your distance (provided you are not required to complete follow-up by your profession). It is okay not to follow up. You have already played an important, and often emotionally demanding, role in the individual's road to recovery; it is okay to refrain from further contact if you feel uneasy.

HOW TO CONTINUE TO HELP

If, after giving thought to the aforementioned considerations, you find it appropriate to have additional contact with the young adult you have assisted, we offer the following suggestions for ways in which you may be able to maximize the impact of additional interactions. In addition, even though in some cases, young adults with psychosis may not be open to treatment at the present time, a number of the ways that we suggest offering support can be helpful to individuals who are not presently in treatment. We encourage you to consider the unique situation of the young adult you are supporting and how these suggestions might apply to you. See Table 5.2 for a summary of these various options.

Practical Support

Young adults with psychosis face a number of hardships in their efforts to access treatment. And, let us be completely honest here, it would be understandable that a young adult in such circumstances would look for any reason to cancel an appointment or avoid a treatment setting. However, providing supports to remove these obstacles increases the likelihood that he or she will engage in treatment. Often, these logistical hardships are helpful targets by which supportive others can assist, as they sometimes are not able to be targeted by treatment providers. For instance, many young adults may not have consistent or reliable access to transportation. Offering to assist with transportation to and from appointments or to pick up prescriptions can help to support the person in being able to make the best use of his or her treatment resources.

Furthermore, in Chapter 2, we discussed a number of cognitive symptoms that occur in the presence of psychosis, one of the most notable being impairment in various types of memories. Supportive others are a valuable resource in assisting a young adult with psychosis to remember the many tasks associated with the treatment. For instance, you could

TABLE 5.2
Supportive Follow-Up Options

Considerations	• Professional limitations and obligations • Your experience and training • Requests of the individual • Your comfort with follow-up contact

Practical support	• Assistance with transportation needs
	• Assistance with remembering treatment-related obligations
	  o Appointments
	  o Medication
	  o Items the young person may want to discuss with providers
	• Helping to identify additional supportive people

Emotional support	• Modeling a positive attitude about mental health treatment • Showing interest in treatment activities • Modeling a nonstigmatizing, blame-free perspective on mental illness • Assisting with finding credible resources about mental illness and treatment

Connecting to additional resources	• Helping to investigate local resources
	• National Alliance on Mental Illness (NAMI)
	• Hearing Voices Network (HVN)
	• Substance abuse supports
	  o Alcoholics Anonymous (AA)
	  o Narcotics Anonymous (NA)
	  o Marijuana Anonymous (MA)

assist the person in setting a daily alarm on his or her cell phone as a reminder to take medications, creating a calendar of appointments, or getting him or her a pocket notebook to write down things to discuss with his or her therapist.

Additionally, supportive others can assist in helping the young person identify other people in his or her life who may be able to provide support in different contexts. For example, it might be helpful to assist the individual in identifying family, friends, trusted teachers, allies at work, or other people in his or her life who might be able to offer support in different ways. As a supportive other, you can help the young person identify his or her allies in recovery and help the young person brainstorm how each person might be able to lend support.

Emotional Support

Seeking mental health treatment is often a stressful experience. This is likely to be particularly true for young adults experiencing psychosis. For some individuals, it is their first contact with mental health providers and so they may have little idea of what to expect, or their ideas may be largely influenced by what they have seen on television or in the movies, or read in books. These are often an unflattering, out-of-date, or altogether inaccurate portrayal of mental health services. As we discussed earlier, this unease is often compounded by the very nature of psychotic symptoms. Individuals may experience general mistrust or paranoia about others, which is likely to extend to mental health professionals. As a supportive other in the life of a young person with psychosis, you have a unique opportunity to help to foster a sense of alliance and trust with mental health providers.

This may take a variety of forms, such as modeling a positive attitude about mental health treatment in general or sharing positive comments about experiences with the mental health system. Although this could mean sharing a personal anecdote about involvement with the system ("I saw a counselor for a while when I was having a rough time. It was pretty helpful"), this is not essential. There are fewer personal ways to model openness and hopefulness about treatment. For instance, if you assist the individual in calling and making an appointment, even a brief comment about the receptionist or intake coordinator on the other end of the phone could be impactful ("He sounded really nice," if indeed he did). The purpose of such comments is to plant a seed of positivity in the face of the difficult challenges the individual is facing. If you are able to model hopefulness and positivity, the young adult will be more likely to adopt that sentiment as well. Furthermore, although mental health treatment is a confidential and often highly private experience, some individuals may find it to be supportive for others to take an interest in their treatment. It also provides an opportunity for the individuals to share concerns and seek reassurance about their engagement in treatment—for instance, asking "How was your first appointment?" or "Are you meeting any cool people at the program?" Of course, this is a sensitive area and it is important that questions do not target details of treatment. As well, it is important to follow the lead of the individual in how much he or she might want to share.

Similarly, it is important to model a nonstigmatizing, blame-free perspective on mental illness. Often, individuals who experience mental health issues, such as psychosis, feel a sense of shame and guilt, and blame themselves for what has happened. Having supportive others in their lives who demonstrate a nonstigmatizing perspective of mental illness can help to combat additional self-blame and guilt. This, too, can come in a variety of forms—for instance, general comments normalizing the need to seek professional psychiatric help, such as "Lots of people get help for lots of different problems" or "Sometimes we all need a hand with things."

As we mentioned previously, the act of seeking mental health services is often fraught with anxiety, misconceptions, and doubts. One way that a supportive other can encourage individuals seeking services is by helping to organize concerns and seek information. For instance, you might suggest that you could help them to create a list of questions they would like to ask their doctor or therapist at the next appointment. In a similar vein, many individuals may turn to the Internet in order to answer their questions about mental health, medications, treatment, and prognosis. Although there is a wealth of information on these topics, much of it is not peer reviewed, meaning that it could be written by anyone with access to an Internet connection and a working keyboard. Therefore, another way to provide support could be to assist the individual in accessing trustworthy sources of information.

Supporting Connections With Additional Resources

Often, even if a young adult has actively engaged in psychiatric treatment, it is helpful to identify additional organizations that can provide information and support. There are a number of organizations dedicated to raising awareness and creating a supportive network for people with mental illnesses. In Chapter 6 of this text, we provide a list of suggested resources on a variety of topics. Here, we discuss several of the national organizations that offer such opportunities. However, there are likely to be a number of additional local resources depending on the area in which you live. Often, mental health providers (even if you are not a patient of their clinic) or the state department of mental health will be happy to provide information on additional local resources.

The National Alliance on Mental Illness (NAMI) is a national organization dedicated to advocacy and education about mental illness. It is well known for initiatives to reduce stigma and raise awareness about mental health issues. NAMI has branches across the country that are dedicated to these issues on a local level. NAMI sponsors a number of resources such as support groups, family education groups, charity events, and educational functions that offer an opportunity for individuals with mental illnesses to connect with one another and increase their knowledge base about their illnesses. The NAMI website provides an easy-to-navigate directory of local NAMI chapters and their related resources.

Similarly, the Hearing Voices Network (HVN) is a growing organization dedicated to normalizing the experience of abnormalities in perception that occur for individuals with psychosis. HVN offers a variety of electronic resources on perceptual abnormalities and a directory of support groups in various areas. Their goal is to provide a context in which individuals who experience voices or visions are able to openly speak about their experiences without shame or judgment.

As we have noted in previous chapters, it is not uncommon for individuals who experience psychosis to self-medicate or use substances to distract from symptoms. A primary concern, however, is that many substances can result in an increase in symptom severity or even precipitate an episode in a person who is relatively stable. In cases in which an individual is willing, peer-run substance use programs such as Smart Recovery, Alcoholics Anonymous (AA), Narcotics Anonymous (NA), and Marijuana Anonymous (MA) can offer adjunctive support for individuals who are making efforts to maintain sobriety. Many of these programs also offer online meetings when an individual is unable to make it to a face-to-face meeting. Of note, these organizations often have identified meetings for young people, where the content is geared toward a younger audience and attendees are closer in age. There are also meetings specialized to men, women, and LGBTQ (lesbian, gay, bisexual, transgender, queer) issues. Each of these organizations has an easy-to-navigate national website that allows you to find local resources.

Processing Your Own Reactions

Although we hope that most people will find the act of assisting a young adult with psychosis to be a meaningful and gratifying experience, we do not want to discount the challenges it may present and the variety of emotional responses that might follow. First, we want to acknowledge the distress, confusion, and uncertainty that may occur when interacting with an individual with psychosis for the first time. Despite attempts to prepare (e.g., reading this text), the reality of interacting with an individual experiencing psychosis is likely to be different than expected. It can be distressing and confusing to try to follow a disorganized conversation, or to interact with someone who is extremely paranoid or fearful. The task you are taking on is not an easy one. There are no clear-cut right or wrong answers, and this can often feel unsettling.

A second reaction that is common is the feeling of not having done enough. This may be particularly true if the individual you were trying to help was not able to successfully connect with services, or if he or she reacted unfavorably to your attempts at intervention. We want to assure you that even if you do not immediately see a result, your show of empathy and support for a young adult who is struggling does make a difference. For individuals experiencing psychosis, there may be many people in their lives with whom they do not have positive interactions; therefore, the opportunity to have an interaction with someone who is able to show care and support is valuable. That said, it is natural to examine the situation and consider what could have been better. Being critical of your performance in such a situation may be helpful, in that it may help you to understand what you might do differently next time. However, it is important to acknowledge your strengths as well. Perhaps, you did an exceptional job of showing empathy, or you resisted the urge to try to convince the person that his or her delusions are not real. These are challenging skills that deserve acknowledgment.

A third reaction may be the feeling that you did not make the right choice in trying to intervene. Although ideally the crisis intervention process would be well received, treatment initiated, and the adolescent or young adult recover, this may not be the case. For example, your engagement may initiate many negative feelings from the individual of concern and/or his or her family. Or the treatment engagement process may be less than successful and many barriers or obstacles are introduced. Finally, your response may have initiated a hospitalization, which can be a very upsetting experience albeit necessary in some cases. There will be many outcomes that will be out of your control and interactions and "next steps" may not go as planned. However, that does not diminish your intention, and the intention of this text. In order to process your reactions, we would like to offer the following suggestions:

DISCUSS THE EXPERIENCE

Share your experience and your feelings about it with someone you trust, perhaps a supervisor or trusted colleague. This may be particularly helpful if the person has had a similar experience or is aware of the challenges of such a situation. Talking through your experience with someone you trust can help you to examine the situation more objectively. In addition, it allows you the opportunity to receive support in a difficult situation. In some ways, this is a "practice what you preach" opportunity for you to model the value of asking for support and assistance when it is needed. Of course, it is important to consider confidentiality and privacy policies, if you are in a position that imposes them, in discussing any information about a young adult you have assisted.

CONNECT WITH A NAMI OR OTHER SUPPORT GROUP

As discussed previously, NAMI is a national organization with resources spread throughout the country, and is one option for finding such resources. It offers a variety of supports for individuals who care about someone with a mental illness. These resources may come in a variety of forms: in-person or online support groups, written materials, seminars, and workshops. These resources will allow you to connect with other individuals who have a mental illness themselves, care about someone with such an illness, or both. In any case, it provides a context to discuss issues related to mental health and receive support from others who may have similar experiences.

SUMMARY

We hope that we have provided considerations and outcomes that will assist in achieving a result that feels helpful and successful to all involved in the interaction. There is nothing easy about the final steps we have outlined here, or the series of steps and guidelines described throughout the text. Psychosis can be a difficult experience for the person living with the symptoms, and also for anyone involving with helping or supporting someone with a psychotic illness. That is true for the most stable patients, but even more so for those who are in the acute stages of a psychotic episode. That is why it is so important to focus on different types of factors that increase the likelihood that an intervention experience is as supportive as possible. We hope that you found this information useful and we encourage you consider the tremendous opportunity you have to alter or improve the trajectory of a young person with a psychotic illness toward recovery.

CHAPTER **SIX**

National Resources

Active Minds

www.activeminds.org

Nonprofit dedicated to student mental health. Active Minds has chapters at many colleges and universities, and a directory can be found on its website. It also offers many resources for individuals with mental illnesses and allies.

Alcoholics Anonymous (AA)

www.aa.org

Peer-based alcohol abuse program with many meetings in nearly every community nationwide as well as online. Use the directory to find meetings in your area.

American Foundation for Suicide Prevention

www.afsp.org

An organization devoted to providing advocacy and supportive resources related to suicide prevention. Its website provides information about local chapters as well as a wealth of information about how to support someone who may be experiencing suicidal thoughts.

American Psychiatric Association

www.psychiatry.org

Although this is an organization for psychiatric providers, its website has a section of information for the public. There, it provides concise and valuable information about a variety of mental health conditions and related topics.

American Psychological Association (APA)

www.apa.org/topics/schiz

APA is a national organization for psychologists that is also dedicated to improving public access to information and services related to psychology. The web address mentioned provides information about schizophrenia as well as information on how to access treatment and additional resources.

Hearing Voices Network

www.hearingvoicesusa.org

An international organization devoted to providing information and to normalizing the experiences of individuals who hear voices.

Marijuana Anonymous (MA)

www.marijuana-anonymous.org

Peer-based marijuana abuse program with many meetings in nearly every community nationwide as well as online. Use the directory to find meetings in your area.

Mental Health America

www.mentalhealthamerica.net

A national community-based nonprofit organization with a global focus on mental wellness. Recent initiatives have focused specifically on early intervention in mental illness.

MentalHealth.gov

www.mentalhealth.gov

A government website that provides a directory of government mental health programs as well as general information related to mental health.

Narcotics Anonymous (NA)

www.na.org

Peer-based narcotics abuse program with many meetings in nearly every community nationwide as well as online. Use the directory to find meetings in your area.

National Alliance on Mental Illness (NAMI)

www.nami.org

A national mental health organization devoted to improving the lives of individuals with mental illnesses and their families. NAMI provides numerous resources and has local chapters in nearly every major city and many smaller communities as well.

National Federation of Families for Children's Mental Health
www.ffcmh.org
A national, family-run organization advocating for the mental health care needs of children and families.

National Institute of Mental Health (NIMH)
www.nimh.nih.gov
A leader in national mental health research. The NIMH website has information about a variety of mental disorders as well as information about their current research initiatives and national educational and outreach events.

National Resource Center for Hispanic Mental Health
www.nrchmh.org
A national nonprofit organization aimed at reducing mental health care disparities in Hispanic communities. It offers a variety of resources in both English and Spanish on its website.

National Suicide Prevention Lifeline
www.suicidepreventionlifeline.org
1-800-273-TALK (8255)
A national suicide prevention resource with a 24-hour, toll-free, confidential suicide prevention hotline available to anyone in suicidal crisis or emotional distress.

OK2TALK
ok2talk.org
An online support community for young adults living with mental illness. Community members are supported in sharing and learning from the stories of others in a stigma-free environment. Resources are available in both English and Spanish.

SMART Recovery
www.smartrecovery.org
A national addiction recovery program aimed at building skills that help to combat addictive behaviors offering meetings in many communities as well as online. This program is often informally differentiated from the "anonymous" programs by having no religious or faith-based emphasis to treatment.

StrengthofUs

strengthofus.org

An online support community for young adults living with mental illness. It offers a variety of informational resources as well as a supportive community environment.

Substance Abuse and Mental Health Services Administration (SAMHSA)

www.samhsa.gov

SAMHSA National Helpline: 1-800-662-HELP (4357)

A division of the Department of Health and Human Services devoted to reducing the impact of behavioral health conditions and addictions on U.S. communities.

Suicide Prevention Resource Center

www.sprc.org

A federally supported center devoted to providing training and resources to prevent suicide. They offer helpful tips and strategies related to suicide prevention for the public.

TeenMentalHealth.org

teenmentalhealth.org

An organization that creates and disseminates mental health literature aimed at teens and young adults. It offers a wealth of jargon-free, engaging resources in formats that are especially designed for young people.

World Health Organization

www.who.int/mental_health

This international organization is devoted to coordinating international health care efforts in conjunction with the United Nations. A section of its website is devoted to mental health conditions and provides information on many mental health conditions, mental health policy, and crisis intervention.

Index

abnormal motor behavior, 48–49
academic performance, 52–53, 97
Active Minds, 155
acute crisis situations, 92
Adderall, 57, 58
additional resources, supporting
connections with, 151–152,
155–158
affective symptoms, 7, 32, 42–47
anxiety, 46–47
depression, 42–44
mania, 44–46
aggression, 65–66, 76, 92, 99, 115
agitation, 48–49
alcohol, 10, 57, 58, 108
Alcoholics Anonymous (AA),
152, 155
alogia, 39
American Foundation for Suicide
Prevention, 155
American Psychiatric Association, 155
American Psychological Association
(APA), 156
anger, 18, 55, 65–66, 76, 94, 115
anhedonia, 39
antidepressants, 15
antipsychotic medications. *See*
medications
anxiety, 12, 21, 46–47, 57, 65, 73, 79,
109, 111, 115
anxiolytics (antianxiety)
medications, 15
asociality, 39–40

assisting. *See also* early intervention;
follow-up; help; intervention plan
as an event, 139
as a process, 139
at-risk individuals, identifying, 2, 5, 25,
113–115
attention, impairment in, 47, 49, 53,
58–59
auditory hallucinations, 36, 89
attention deficit, 58
paranoia, 63
responding to internal stimuli, 55,
56, 98
authority versus nonauthority figure,
70–71
avolition, 38–39

behavior, changes in, 7, 52. *See
also* concerning behaviors;
engagement behavior;
problematic behaviors; unsafe/
bizarre behaviors; unusual
behavior
"better safe than sorry" approach,
3, 25, 52, 60, 91, 103, 113,
116, 147
biological triggers, 10
bipolar disorder with psychotic
features
prevalence rate, 9
symptoms, 9
body language, 75
broken arm analogy, 1, 3

CPSIA information can be obtained
at www.ICGtesting.com
Printed in the USA
FFOW01n1309230217
32796FF

9 780826 124371